320349 CC
1956

The author writing under the pseudonym of Dr Robert Clifford, is a general practitioner in a Berkshire village. Here he successfully combines medical practice with writing and broadcasting.

A Yorkshireman by birth, he is married with three children.

Surely Not, Doctor!

DR ROBERT CLIFFORD

Illustrated by Larry

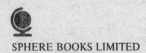

SPHERE BOOKS LIMITED

First published in Great Britain by
Pelham Books Limited 1985
Text copyright © by Dr Robert D. Clifford 1985
Illustrations copyright © by Larry 1985
Published by Sphere Books Ltd 1986
27 Wright's Lane, London W8 5SW

For Pam, Trevor, Paul, Gill and Jane

Printed and bound in Great Britain by
Collins, Glasgow

Contents

Prologue

Life is a tragedy, for we are all born eventually to die. We survive our tragedies by laughing at them.

A friend once told me that when he was under the influence of ether he dreamed he was turning over the pages of a great book, in which he knew he would find, on the last page, the meaning of life.

The pages of the book were alternately tragic and comic, and he turned page after page, his excitement growing, not only because he was approaching the answer, but because he couldn't know, until he arrived, on which side of the book the final page would be. At last it came: the universe opened up to him in a hundred words: and they were uproariously funny.

He came back to consciousness crying with laughter, remembering everything. He opened his lips to speak. It was then that the great and comic answer plunged back out of his reach.

Christopher Fry

CHAPTER 1

Toeing the Line

Glancing from the bedroom window of a bronchitic patient whose chest I had just been examining, I noticed, on the lawn of the bungalow next door, a man who seemed to be sitting by some sort of red fountain which was spraying over the grass and his idle lawnmower.

I watched the scene blankly for a moment or two before I realised exactly what was happening. The red fountain was blood . . . and it was coming from the man's foot. For once it looked as though I might be in the right place at the right time.

I shot downstairs and ran into the garden, vaulting the fence into the next-door garden which belonged to the bungalow of Jack Johnson-Peel, a leading London publisher who used the bungalow as a summer residence.

Jack was sitting in the middle of his lawn as if mesmerised, looking at the toe of his left shoe, out of which an intermittent stream of blood was spraying the surrounding turf and lawnmower.

'Good heavens, Jack!' I said, 'what have you done?'

'It's this new rotamower,' said Jack, still watching the fountain and looking rather disappointed as I applied firm pressure with my grubby handkerchief, stopping the brilliant red cascade.

He said, 'I was trying it out for the first time. I've just realised that where it says "place foot here", you should put your foot on top and not underneath.'

Momentarily I lifted my handkerchief off his foot and blood gushed out again. There was just a gap where his big toe should have been; he had taken it clean off at the junction with the foot.

Suddenly there was a shriek from the house and out rushed his wife Penny, who had woken from her afternoon nap to see her husband lying flat on the lawn, blood all over the place and somebody clutching his foot.

'Good God, Jack!' she cried. 'I told you not to fool about with mechanical things! You don't know the first thing about them. What's he done and what have we got to do, Doctor Bob?'

'If you can get me some strapping and some clean linen, we can tidy up his foot,' I said. 'We will have to get him to hospital and I'll get Henry, my partner, to see him. And we must pick up his toe. There's a good chance we'll be able to get it stuck back on – it's a fairly clean cut.'

It took only a few minutes to get things sorted out, the foot dressed, and the bleeding staunched. All we needed now was the toe, which was nowhere in sight.

'Pack him off in the car straight away, Penny,' I said. 'We've got to be quick. I'll bring the toe along as soon as I find it.'

I helped Jack into the car and then made a minute search of the garden; the toe surely couldn't have gone far. It would certainly be covered with blood – there seemed to be pints of it about – but what might have been a toe turned out to be a pebble. I searched and searched but could find nothing. I couldn't believe it: toes don't just vanish.

I was distracted by a movement in the bushes. I went over to find Jack Johnson-Peel's beagle chewing happily at what I could imagine was his first human toe. When I tried to wrest it

2

from him, I was met with a most fearsome growl. A couple of seconds later, the problem was solved: with two quick gulps he had swallowed the lot. Anything they offered the dog for dinner was going to be small beer after this. This was going to be very difficult.

I got in my car and drove to the hospital to find Henry, my surgical partner, all scrubbed up ready to operate.

'Did you find the missing link, Bob my lad?' he said.

'No,' I said. 'Um . . . er . . . I think it must have been shattered to bits by the mower. Perhaps absolutely disintegrated.' Which, in the true sense of the word, it had.

'Right,' said Henry. 'Then we'll just tidy him up.' And Jack Johnson-Peel was wheeled off to the operating theatre to have the amputation area patched up.

They kept him in hospital for about four days and I came to see him the first day he was home. He was sitting with his foot up in a chair. The chair was almost in the place of his

accident. A rounded semi-circle of luxuriant growth which marked the outlines of the lawnmower and the area that the blood had sprayed on, showed that, whatever else Jack Johnson-Peel was made of, some of him was a very good fertiliser.

I made a point of dressing his foot myself. This would normally be a job for the district nurse but I reasoned that (a) he didn't live too far away from me, (b) I enjoyed his company and he was a most distinguished and well-known publisher and (c) the job wasn't a great deal of trouble.

But subconsciously the real reason was that he was the managing director of a famous publishing house . . . and one day, who knows, he might well consider publishing a book of mine.

I visited him and dressed his foot daily for ten days. Sometimes he was sitting out in the garden and at other times, when the weather wasn't so good, he was inside. But every time I visited him his beagle sat obediently and devotedly by his side. On my tenth visit, as I was finishing the dressing, in came Penny.

'Look at this,' I said. 'The master and his dog. What a picture, almost a Landseer.'

'It's funny you should say that,' said Penny. 'Bozer is really my dog. Jack's never liked him very much and the dog's never had much to do with Jack. But it just shows how intelligent he is. He knows Jack's hurt and can't get about, so he sits by him, guarding him; he must have been very fond of him after all. In fact, he's never left his side since the accident.'

'Yes,' I said. 'There's very little doubt that he has a great liking for him . . .'

CHAPTER 2

Water, Water Everywhere

I was the fourth partner in a group of five in a little Somerset town called Tadchester. Tadchester (population 6,500) stands on the estuary of the River Tad, in one of the most beautiful parts of the Somerset coast. It is a market town, with some fishing, some light industry, and a great deal of farming.

The town is split in two by the River Tad, and further split by the large hill which dominates one side of the river. The other side of the river is flat pastureland, stretching off to marshes and the sea coast. You are not just a Tadchester resident – you are strictly Up-the-Hill or Down-the-Hill.

We were the only general practice in the town, and also took care of the local hospital. The five partners each had his own area of responsibility at the hospital: Steve Maxwell, the senior partner, had a special interest in medicine; Henry Johnson, the second senior, was the surgeon; Jack Hart, the third partner, was the anaesthetist; I, as the fourth partner, was reckoned to be the expert on midwifery and was pretty good at piercing ears; and Ron Dickinson, the fifth and junior partner – an accomplished athlete who spent a great deal of his time running, jumping, swimming, sailing and water ski-ing – was our ENT specialist and removed the local tonsils. We were a happy and well-balanced team.

When I first came to Tadchester there were great social divisions between Up-the-Hill and Down-the-Hill. By and large those living Up-the-Hill tended to be the Have-nots and those living Down-the-Hill the Haves. Of course there were exceptions on both sides of the river. After the coal mine had shut, various light industries began to appear in Tadchester: most of these, apart from the plastics factory which was near the coal mine, were built Up-the-Hill and they attacted with them new and more expensive housing and a growing population. This in no way diminished the rivalry between the two halves of the town, in fact, if anything, it increased it. It was almost like two sides having equal weaponry.

A landmark Up-the-Hill was St Peter's church, and the Victorian forefathers of Tadchester must have anticipated that one day there would be a population boom there. In 1870, or more accurately between 1870 and 1875, they built a church only slightly smaller than the Parish Church of St Mary's. Where St Mary's served a large congregation in the town, St Peter's, certainly at the time of its building, covered a very sparsely populated area.

The incumbent at St Peter's church was the Reverend Darch. There were few people who could remember Tadchester without him. He came there as a curate at the age of twenty-three, never marrying but remaining faithfully wedded to St Peter's for a further sixty years.

He was an old and confused man when I first came to Tadchester, and time certainly didn't improve him. He was the only man I've ever known, fishermen included, who continually wore rubber gum boots day in, day out, summer or winter, at church or cocktail party.

As far as I could gather, he had always worn gum boots. They were not related to his present disability, namely that he had very little control over his waterworks. Whenever he saw running water or heard the sound of splashing, he was unable to prevent himself joining in. This was particularly bad at christenings when he had to splash water over infants' heads. He was always completely unaware of his own contribution to

6

the service and the trail of water from the font back to the pulpit was holy water of a unique kind. Whatever he originally wore his gum boots for, they were now an essential part of his equipment.

He drifted around in a private and cosy haze, and was famous for an incident during his eighties when, at one winter's evensong, remembering that he'd left his car outside with its lights on, he asked his congregation to kneel in silent prayer. Then he nipped out of the pulpit, got into his car and drove home.

His sermons were unintelligible and there had been constant pressure from the parishioners for him to be moved. At their bidding, I suggested many a time that perhaps he should take things more easily, but he would hear nothing of it.

'Plenty of work in me yet, Doctor,' he would say in his booming voice. 'Plenty of the Lord's work still to do.'

Without the support of two industrious lay preachers the church would have folded. He always refused to have a curate, claiming that he had managed on his own quite well for sixty years so there was no need to have anybody else. He was quite impervious to hints.

Eventually he became such a passenger, such an embarrassment to his church and the community that the Church Council wrote to the bishop, pleading with him to ask the Reverend Darch to resign, or even to sack him. The bishop, who was always reluctant to take this sort of step, but knowing that church ministers usually take the hint, wrote a firm letter to the Reverend Darch. He thanked him for his services in the past and pointed out that the church, the body of the church, the head of the church and all the church, felt that the time had come for him to retire.

The response was a letter from the Reverend Darch saying: 'Dear Bishop, When your predecessor' – and he named a bishop fifty years back – 'first appointed me, I had no idea that my position here was only a temporary one.'

Things were at an impasse. There seemed no solution until fate took a hand.

Sadly, but mercifully, two months after the bishop's letter, the Reverend Darch absentmindedly stepped out in front of his car. He was knocked down by a lorry and killed instantly.

Ron Dickinson and I arrived at the scene of the accident, both about the same time. There was Reverend Darch lying crumpled at the side of the road, gum boots sticking out at right angles to the gutter, with a puzzled smile on his face as if he was wondering, 'Did I jump or was I pushed?' An enigma to the end.

'The poor old lad's got one consolation,' said Ron Dickinson as we tidied him up while waiting for the ambulance. 'At least he died with his boots on.'

CHAPTER 3

Warm Hearts

Times were changing at the surgery. Although Gladys, our senior receptionist, still reigned supreme she was muttering about retirement. Her sidekick, the ever loquacious Grace, had been saying it was her last year for some years, and, alas, none of us was getting any younger. Ron Dickinson, our junior partner, was the only new medical face in the practice since I had joined. The pattern of medicine was changing; the hospital had almost completely gone. Henry would soon reach the age when he would be retired as a surgeon and there would no longer be a surgeon at all in Tadchester. Already he was reduced to mainly casualty surgery work, many of the hospital beds having been taken over for the care of the elderly. The midwifery unit was now at the nearby town of Winchcombe, apart from the odd case dealt with at home. When I had first come into the practice I could reckon on three home deliveries a fortnight. Now, if I got two or three a year, I was lucky and they were becoming so rare that I had almost forgotten the routine procedure. Fortunately our midwife, the ever-faithful Nurse Plank, was still in practice and she took charge of the whole situation.

We had a variety of staff coming and going at the surgery.

Young girls arriving, marrying, having babies, going, being replaced; an ever-increasing staff as we expanded our facilities with a nurses' treatment room, electrocardiogram unit and so on.

It often took some of our newly trained, highly qualified staff some time to adjust to the idiosyncrasies of our patients. I remember a new dispenser coming to me almost in despair at the end of a heavy day.

'However do I interpret a note like this?' she asked, showing me a crudely written letter that read, 'Grandma says please could she have another bottle of emotion, and not the sort that leaves a lot of sentiment in the bottom of the bottle.'

'That's easy,' I said, recognising the handwriting. 'It means a quart of liquid paraffin for old Mrs Smithson. I'm never sure whether she cooks with it or puts it in her all-night heater. I'm sure she never uses it as a medicine.'

The biggest change had been in the increase in the number of people who had their own transport or who had friends who could transport them. Now we had bigger and more frequent surgeries and did fewer home visits; the home visits being confined to acute medical cases and routine visits to the frail and elderly.

The days when we had twenty-five to thirty visits a day had vanished. If we had a dozen visits a day to do, we thought we were hard pressed. And perhaps we were.

There were many advantages in seeing people in their home environment, but of course there were also many advantages in seeing people in the surgery where you could do so much more for them in the way of investigations and minor nursing and surgical procedures. A few years ago I spent most of my day buzzing around, leaping in and out of my car at a great rate, whereas now I spent most of my time sitting behind my desk.

I don't know if I like this new way of medicine as much.

I still had one clinical attachment at the hospital, where I looked after a medical recovery ward and once a week used to do a round with John Bowler, the physician at Winchcombe, who kept some beds at Tadchester. At the end of his ward round I would sit and glean from him information on all the most recent medical advances, techniques and new drugs.

I kept an appointment free to see one representative from a drug house each week. They would always bring beautifully illustrated magazines, copies of articles, and some gift, like a ballpoint pen or a car windscreen scraper.

Gladys was very much in charge of everything at the practice. Only the outrageous Grace could take liberties with her – even Steve Maxwell was rather frightened – and it was usually Gladys and Grace who decided which patient should see which doctor. We were, of course, not all in surgery at the same time so sometimes we would have directed to us a patient whom we would reckon was not really our 'type'. I always used to say that I was a working-class doctor and to an extent I meant that for, having been a coal miner, I felt I had a better understanding of people who came from industrial or agricultural working backgrounds, than of people who came from the rather more sophisticated ones. But even I, sometimes, had to go out of my class as it were . . .

It is never easy to accept patients who are registered with another doctor. Would-be new patients come in with complaints about their own doctor, but only very occasionally are they justified: there are many more difficult patients, in my experience, than there are bad doctors.

It is important that you are able to communicate with your doctor. If you can't, then you have reasonable grounds for finding somebody else, but it is very difficult, having been registered with one doctor, to get another to accept you: you're under suspicion.

One day I noticed among the pile of cards on my desk, a plain slip saying 'New Private Patient' from Winchcombe. I asked Grace about it when she came in to tidy up the desk before I started my surgery. 'You've got a real toff there, Doctor Bob,' she said, as only Grace can say without causing offence. 'She's a Right Hon. You're moving up in society.'

I couldn't think of any reason why somebody who had lived

in Winchcombe, which had excellent doctors and lots and lots of them, should want to travel at least twelve miles to Tadchester to see me. I looked forward to meeting this Right Hon. with interest. She had booked a double appointment, again another ominous sign; it meant she had a lot to talk about.

I visualised a hawk-faced, dominant lady who had worn out every doctor in Winchcombe and now wanted to tell me the story of her life. When the turn of the Right Hon. came, I was pleasantly surprised. She was an extremely smart and very nice lady of about forty-five. Her name had rung a bell somewhere, and as she sat down I remembered that she was a magistrate in Winchcombe.

I'm not always very good at assessing people; I can often make the most terrible mistakes. But this lady did not seem at all like a disgruntled patient. Here she was, however, obviously having explored the medical situation in her own vicinity and travelling twelve miles for another opinion.

'What can we do to help you?' I said, smiling. 'You've come a long way.'

'Yes, thank you, Doctor,' she said, 'there are one or two things I'm worried about. If you could give me a general overhaul, I would be exceedingly grateful.'

My heart sank. Patients who want complete overhauls present problems: it's not just physically possible on the National Health, not without presenting some symptoms. But this lady was private and she'd booked double time.

'I'm afraid I'll have to ask you what brings you over to Tadchester,' I said. 'There are so many good doctors in Winchcombe. Can you tell me what happened?'

'Nothing's happened, Doctor. I have no complaints about them at all. I have heard that you are sympathetic and will listen to people. I don't really want to go into the matter too deeply but I would be most grateful if you could see me today and possibly continue to look after me. I can assure you that I don't ever expect you to come and visit me.'

It was very unusual for a patient who was changing doctors

not to have some criticism. She looked slightly embarrassed about it all and I did wonder – for she was certainly attractive – whether she and her doctor had got too close to each other and felt it better for both if she were medically looked after elsewhere. But the Right Hon. didn't look as if she dillied and dallied and it's difficult to do anything in the Tadchester/Winchcombe area without everybody knowing.

We got down to her medical problems. They seemed minor: she had a slight difficulty in holding her urine – she passed water when she coughed and sneezed; she had a bit of a cold. She said that no doctor had examined her fully (and this was without innuendo) for some time. She was anxious about blood pressure and one thing and another.

I told her to go to the examination room, get undressed, and I would come and see her.

I had a good look at her. Her chest was clear, blood pressure normal, nothing in her abdomen. She did have a degree of prolapse of the muscles that supported her womb. It might be helped by exercises but would probably need a repair operation sometime, although it wasn't essential.

I told her to get dressed and asked if she could manage a specimen of water. With a blood test and chest X-ray arranged she would have had a really good five-thousand-mile service. I saw another patient and then the Right Hon. came in with the urine specimen. Obviously she'd been crying.

'Look', I said, 'I don't want to pry, but clearly something's been upsetting you. What's the matter?'

'I'm crying with relief,' she said. 'It's you. Thank God I've found you.'

'Why?' I said. 'What's so marvellous about me?'

'It sounds so silly,' she said, 'but . . . you have warm hands. I cannot bear anybody touching me with cold hands, particularly in the more intimate places. If anybody puts a cold hand on me I react in the same way most people do if they have their feet tickled. I scream and wriggle like a schoolgirl – I just can't help it. And I've not found a doctor yet with warm hands.'

'I've had all sorts of worries about my health – I'm sure they have been groundless – but I literally daren't go to a doctor locally. I know there is this strong medical code of complete confidentiality, but who could resist telling somebody in confidence how I screech and scream as soon as they lay a hand on me?

'I can just imagine sitting on the Bench with everybody sniggering at me. It's like one of the town councillors at Winchcombe said: "It's not we who break the confidences of the Council, it's the people we tell in confidence who let all the secrets out." '

'Well my hands are usually cold,' I confessed. 'You know what they say, "Cold hands, warm heart." I don't know why they're warm this morning – I must have had them in my pockets.'

'Thank God they were,' said the Right Hon. 'I was just about at my wits' end. I was thinking I would have to go to Taunton every time I had a sore throat. What's happened now is that I've broken the ice, literally and metaphorically. I know I can come to you and say, "Now don't forget, I'm the one who can't bear cold hands." Thank you so much for seeing me. I will accept your advice and see a gynaecologist and, if I may, whenever I'm worried, about anything medical, come and see you again.'

'I promise,' I said, 'that I'll keep our secret and I won't tell anybody about it, even in confidence.'

She smiled. She knew and I knew that even the fact that she was travelling from Winchcombe to Tadchester just to see a general practitioner, would have tongues wagging in a country district like ours. It would put my status up but both she and I could bear that. Thus are reputations made.

* * *

In Tadchester reputations could actually be lost in a flash!

The death of the Reverend Darch was not the end of the troubles for St Peter's. A brand new, progressive young vicar was appointed and a grand summer party was held to

introduce him to his flock at the house of the Gentrys – Mr Gentry being the senior sidesman at St Peter's.

There must have been fifty or sixty people in the large room that overlooked the lawn with a view across the estuary. It was a hot summer's day and most of the women were in backless, strapless types of dress, including the big-bosomed Mrs Gentry who, rather overcome by being hostess to such a large gathering, was laughing more loudly than she should at any minor witticism of the new vicar.

During one outburst of laughter, with her head pulled back to give better volume to her appreciation, she failed to notice that the right-hand one of her magnificent two had popped out over her dress. The quick-witted young vicar had the situation in hand in a second.

'Quick everybody,' he said, 'look out of the window!'

Everybody turned at his dramatic appeal. He didn't actually lift up and replace the offending article, but he was able to indicate to Mrs Gentry that some of her laughter was out of place. He then turned to join the rest of his flock, who were gazing out on to the immaculate lawn, in the middle of which were an Alsatian and an Airedale, making love in the only way dogs know how.

CHAPTER 4

Family Affairs

We had waved our eldest son Trevor goodbye to Kingston Polytechnic. He had the usual problems settling in, ringing home most nights to begin with but gradually settling down. Before going to Kingston he had been a shy boy, awkward in manner, who always kept in the background, and I think his first year, although he never said so, was rather difficult. He did have some fun: he played his trumpet in the band at the Christmas pantomime. He also joined one or two clubs, one of which was a completely new activity for him: amateur dramatics. (My first date with Pam, my darling wife, was to see her in the Fetcham Players, so perhaps acting was in the blood.)

After an unsettled period, in the early part of the second year when he wondered whether he wanted to go on with the course, he became very enthusiastic about acting. As proud, and greatly surprised, parents we went up to see him take the lead in *The Threepenny Opera* which, after its run in Kingston, went on to a Student Drama Festival in Paris. Since his choirboy days we had no idea Trevor could sing, and acting – this completely new venture – became his first love. The student company toured Cornwall in the holidays and our retiring son who used to shun the limelight, now became very much more extroverted, full of life and confidence, highly organised with everything: money, clothes and studies, all worked out to a definite plan. I agreed with his view that you couldn't absorb more than two hours' study a night – after that you were just satisfying your own conscience – and that you were much better getting up and going and doing something else. Even so I was a bit worried about his cavalier attitude to his studies, but in the end, in spite of all his acting, in spite of not doing more than two hours' study a night, and in spite of the fact that he took a larger and larger part in the social life, conducting the orchestra for the pantomime and engaging in all major college activities, he finished with a 2.1 honours degree and nobody in his year did any better than that.

He was also awarded the Law Student Prize. This was for the best all-round student, voted for by the staff and the students themselves. He was thrilled.

If Trevor was organised, his brother Paul (four years his junior) was about as disorganised as he could be, unless it was in dressing himself for some activity. Whichever sport he undertook, he was always perfectly turned out in the appropriate gear. He had a great urge to leave the grammar school and go to the local technical college: you are thought much more of as a man of the world at the tech. and it doesn't have school discipline. So having scraped through a few O-levels, Paul went off to the tech, where he had so many free study periods that he could do all his homework before he came home. I didn't know of any other boy who was doing A-levels who had every evening free, but Trevor had managed to do well in his degree with his own regime, so perhaps Paul was the same.

Trevor had fallen in love with acting; Paul's passion was music. The Beatles and Rolling Stones were going to be nothing compared to the group he got together. For sheer application they should have been the best in the world. They worked hard, wrote their own music, and practised in our garage until a round robin from the neighbours suggested that they practised elsewhere as the noise of the amplifiers was having an unsettling effect on the foundations of the houses. One neighbour complained, 'I don't mind the boys playing but when I can't hear my own TV set with all the doors and windows closed, I have a feeling they've got to tone things down a bit.'

The group was made up of Paul, Brian, John and Dick – two guitars, bass and drums. The boys had quite a number of local engagements and gradually they got bookings further and further afield. They even made a journey to London and played in the top of Ronnie Scott's Club.

Jane was beside herself. Ronnie Scott's! Why couldn't she go? There were many reasons why I didn't want our young and impressionable daughter unaccompanied in London at night. The only way was for me to go with her, so I trekked up to London to endure five hours of continuous noise and flashing lights that nearly made me blind and stone deaf as

well as being totally confused by the unintelligible words of the songs. I was relieved to catch the three a.m. train with Jane back to quiet Somerset. She loved it. But it was not, as they say, my scene.

What the boys needed was a manager, and they suddenly produced a man who was going to lead them to great things. His first action was to get them involved in the hire purchase of seven thousand pounds' worth of equipment. The HP company arranging the finance said as many people as possible should sign the HP agreement. A friend of the lads, Mick Brown, who was nothing to do with the group and had just popped in for a cup of tea, was inveigled into adding his name to the list of signatures.

'Look, Dad,' said Paul, 'the decision is ours. We're all in this together. We've got to have this good equipment if we're going to get anywhere. The manager's paying his share too. Don't worry – we're going to be famous. We're going to buy houses for all the family eventually.'

The amplifying gear, I think, was really built for the Albert Hall. When the group played for a local concert they could be heard ten miles away.

The manager's reign was short-lived. After three months – and some dispute over whether he'd passed on the boys' instalments to the HP firm – he disappeared. After a further three months, two of the boys dropped out. As I'd feared, in the end Paul and I were left with a bill of about six thousand pounds to pay. Two of the boys chipped in for a time. I took legal advice and the solicitor told me that the best thing was to keep on paying and try to sell the equipment. We had absolutely no success over this – what group of lads could afford six thousand pounds? – and before long the equipment was out of date. For three years I had to pay a hundred pounds a month. Paul, who was working in a garage, still hell-bent on music but just doing something to tide him over until he hit the big time, had to put fifty pounds of his precious wages into paying the thing off. For the last two years of the contract Paul and I were the only ones who made any contribuions at all. When we finished paying the equipment was worth nothing.

At the beginning of his music days Paul had fallen madly in love with Gill, the beautiful blonde-haired daughter of leading jockey Eddie Cracknell, one of whose claims to fame was that he won the first horserace to be shown on BBC TV's 'Grandstand'. Apart from minor attachments, Paul and Gill never had any other boy or girl friends and very soon she became an extra daughter in the family and close friend and confidante of Jane.

Paul's academic record of a few O-levels wasn't anywhere near Trevor's, but he did have one great gift – he was an absolute dab hand at poker. As we forked out the monthly instalments, I couldn't help wishing that the Job Centre would come up with an opening for a riverboat gambler.

'I want to be a musician, Dad, that's all I want,' he said, as members of the group came and went. Paul could write beautiful songs and could sing good ballads but it was the razzamatazz of life in the music business that really interested him. A record company offered to buy his songs but he wouldn't let them go without his group. Gradually, although still a most accomplished musician, he realised that he might have to find other ways to earn his living. He managed to find a job with some prospects with an electronics factory Up-the-Hill, while Gill went on an art and design degree course that took her up to Maidenhead and Southampton. They were now miles apart, but still their friendship flourished.

The children were all growing up far too quickly. What was pleasing was their relationship with each other; they didn't try and rival each other in any way but supported each others' activities. Trevor drove the van when Paul's group went on an unsuccessful tour of the south coast, where he had to be restrained from throttling the manager.

Jane, who had been a model schoolgirl at the local convent, studiously getting all her O-levels, had decided that A-levels must be done somewhere else, and quite emphatically decided that she should go to the comprehensive, formerly the grammar school, for her final two years of schooling.

Jane was young enough to be in a different age group from her brothers. She held them in tremendous awe and was completely spoiled by them. At a party she gave in the church hall, Paul's group provided the music and Paul was general master of ceremonies. Much to Jane's dismay, he shut the party down at ten because some of the boys were getting the worse for drink. As most of the children's parents weren't due to pick them up until eleven, it caused some consternation when they had to stand outside in the cold for an hour. But nobody was going to muck up Paul's younger sister's party, even if he mucked it up himself by shutting it down early.

Although Trevor had left home, we always used to try and manage one week as a family together somewhere: a week in Kent, a week in a farmhouse flat near Evesham, or a week on a boat. Whatever the children's ambitions, and none of them seemed to be quite sure what they wanted, they all knew they would never practise medicine.

'It sounds selfish,' said Trevor, 'but we really don't want to work weekends and nights.'

They were good-humoured, caring children; my wife Pam and I were indeed blessed.

* * *

Pam's father, Gerry, was ailing. He had developed a condition that we knew we could contain for some time but would not be able to stave off forever. Happily his illness did not interfere too much with the last two years of his life but it meant he had to receive blood transfusions from time to time. He had become much more religious in his later years and had a stained-glass window commissioned in memory of Pam's mother in Sticklepath Church in Barnstaple, where they had lived for some years and where Pam's mother, Bill, was much remembered.

Gerry was a great character; a marvellous *bon viveur*. He

loved his fishing and enjoyed a bit of shooting. He raced greyhounds in his younger days and was a great follower of the horses. In his middle years he had several friends who were jockeys. He would probably go to three or four race meetings and back only one horse.

'Only back when you know it's trying,' he used to say. 'You've got to be in the know.'

He was always fully engaged with life. He maintained that his racehorse punting saw his family through the leaner years, and in the very early lean years, as well as doing a job during the day, he played his violin in London theatre orchestras in the evening. He had a great passion for golf but, alas, was never a natural.

After he had lost his wife he fitted in well with the family. The extension he had built on to our house meant that he was always with us but never on top of us. When I look back, I realise how self-contained he was and how much he got out of life with his racing, his work as an engineer, his shooting and fishing, and his music. He held up very well until his last few terminal months, but we were able to keep him at home and in comfort and he died peacefully at home with Pam, myself and the children always near.

There was a memorial service in St Mary's church then Pam, Trevor and I and the vicar of St Mary's travelled over to Winchcombe for a cremation service which the vicar conducted. It was all very nicely and tastefully done. On the way back in the hired car, the vicar, who was rather pompous, said to Trevor, 'Do you remember the last thing your grandfather said to you?'

Trevor hesitated for a moment, and said, 'Yes.'

'Always remember those words,' said the vicar. 'Always remember them.'

Trevor was quiet, embarrassed and strangely silent for the rest of the journey.

We got home and over tea he said to Pam, 'Mum, do you know what Gaga's (the children's name for Gerry) last words to me were?'

'You did look a bit confused when the vicar asked you about them,' said Pam, 'What were they?'

'I couldn't really tell the vicar,' said Trevor, 'that his very last words to me were "What won the Grand National?".'

It was a fitting epitaph.

CHAPTER 5

A Collection of Characters

Albert Coaltart was one of the most patient, meticulous men I knew. His hobby was making models and on the top of my sideboard I have the most beautiful model of a French haycart, accurate in every detail. When Albert came to the surgery he would often bring his latest piece of work to show me: perhaps a minute caravan complete with everything from door hinges to cooking instruments, each hand crafted and often improvised from bits of cocoa tins and such like. Not for Albert the ready-made fixture; he made every part of every model himself. He really could have made a good living from his models, but his pleasure was in making them and I never saw him sell one.

Healthwise he had a chequered history. He had worked for the Ministry of Defence at the waterproofing establishment at Stowyn, involved in underwater work the nature of which he would never divulge – it was classified as Top Secret. This injured his health and he was retired early on medical grounds.

Digging one day on his allotment he strained his back and the resulting back pain spoilt everything for him. I tried most of the anti-inflammatory drugs and pain relievers. He had physiotherapy, saw an orthopaedic surgeon, wore a surgical jacket, but we could not get his back right. Although he kept on with his model-making and kept himself busy, he was slowly but steadily getting more and more depressed. Instead of the smiles and the new models that he brought to the surgery, he would come in hobbling and stand rather than sit while we searched for some new preparation that might help his back.

It didn't really register with me when one day he came in, not smiling but not looking unhappy, and sat straight down. I noticed, however, he was limping a bit.

'How are things today, Albert?'

'Something for the book here, Doctor,' he said. 'I was sitting on the toilet, reading, with the door partly open – the rest of the house were out – when the cat jumped through the lavatory window, onto my knee and made for the door. It scared the wits out of me.

'I aimed to kick it as it went and stubbed my toe on the door. It bled, so I wrapped a handkerchief round it. I searched all over the house, but I couldn't find any dressings, so I decided to go across the common to the shop.'

Albert lived in Elfin Cross, the small hamlet to the west of Tadchester, which consisted of a couple of pubs, a garage, about thirty houses, and a shop that sold everything.

'I was half way across the common,' said Albert, 'when I fell smack, straight on my face. Some kids had put a trip wire across the path, the little beggars. I hardly made it to the shop.'

'Well, let's have a look at the toe, Albert,' I said. 'You do seem to go in for misfortunes in a big way.'

I looked at his badly bruised toe, cleaned it up and put a fresh dressing on it. Then I saw that he was grinning.

'Have you noticed anything, Doctor?'

'No, Albert,' I said.

'That fall has cleared my back – I'm better!'

'Ah ha!' I said, 'this is how new cures are discovered. Perhaps you can get that cat for me. I've got several patients whose backs need sorting out.'

'I don't think the cat would be much use to you, Doctor,' said Albert. 'I'll wring its neck if I find it . . .'

* * *

Penelope Smith was a keep-fit fanatic. She ran the flourishing League of Health and Beauty in Tadchester, and her own private gymnasium. Though an attractive and pleasant personality, she was not being pinned down (as it were) by any admirer until she had reached the age of thirty-two. She was an extremely pleasant lady, believed in what she did, thought rightly that keeping fit was the basis of good health, and always had time to listen to people who wanted to get themselves into better condition. She once even dared to suggest that she might have some exercises that would help me lose weight.

I saw very little of her. I was vaguely aware that she was engaged and about to be married and thought no more about it until I was called urgently to her home one Saturday. She had got out of the bath, her back had locked, and she couldn't stand up properly.

'Is it very painful?' I asked her mother over the phone 'No,' she said, 'but would you come as soon as you can? She's supposed to be getting married at two-thirty today.'

I rushed round to the house to find a small pantomime in progress: Penelope bent double in the bathroom and father and mother wandering around distractedly, muttering 'Tut-tut,' 'Fancy that,' and 'Well, I never . . .'

I do a little bit of manipulating, and so I gave her back a tweak. I offered her some pain relievers and a small dose of tranquilliser. I wondered if part of her problem was anxiety, but whatever it was, my manipulation, the pain relievers and a relaxant would certainly unbend her back. I went away confidently and gave her a ring at about half past twelve to see how things were going.

'She's not much better, Doctor,' said mum.

'Her tablets should be working now,' I said. 'Stand her up and get her moving about slowly.'

There was a frantic phone call at about quarter to one.

'We stood her up, Doctor, and she fainted.'

I rushed round again where the rather slapstick atmosphere of a couple of hours before had changed. The mother wasn't dressed; the father wasn't; the bride hadn't washed her hair; things were getting out of hand. I was in a bit of a fix myself.

Penelope really did seem to be in a lot of pain and well and truly locked in her uncomfortable and undignified position.

'Try sitting her up gently in a chair,' I suggested. 'I think I know of somebody nearby with a wheelchair. I'll go and fetch it. We'll certainly be able to get her into that.'

There was an old lady with Parkinson's disease who lived at the opposite end of the village. She had a marvellous husband who had nursed her and taken care of her for years so I went down and explained the situation to him.

'Could I borrow the wheelchair for a wedding?'

'By all means, Doctor,' he said. 'Good luck to the bride.'

I took the wheelchair back but, by the time I got there, it was a quarter to two. The wedding was due to take place at two-thirty in a village about ten miles away and the bride had decided that her hair must be washed before she went. I gave the most strict instructions that she should be sat in the chair and wheeled to the car. When she got out, she must not try to stand. She must be wheeled into the church and stay in the wheelchair throughout the whole of the ceremony. When they got back from the ceremony, they were to let me know and I'd come and see her.

The couple were flying off somewhere for a honeymoon the next day. It was all terribly sad. I heard no more from the family that day and as I didn't know where the reception was being held, I couldn't make my follow-up visit.

The next morning, around came the beaming father and mother of the bride.

'Thank you for all your help yesterday, Doctor. We got Penelope into the car and when she got to the church she managed to get up and actually walk up the aisle, and by the end of the reception she was well enough to go on her honeymoon.' There were great big pieces of wedding cake both for me and for the old couple who had lent the wheelchair.

Penelope shouldn't have walked, but I don't think she would ever have dared to raise her head at her keep-fit studio if it had been known that she had been wheeled up the aisle in a wheelchair for her wedding.

I heard no details of the honeymoon, but from her sprightly walk and beaming face on her return, she'd obviously had plenty of keep-fit exercise.

* * *

Mrs Tomlinson was nearly raped more often than the rest of all the ladies in my practice put together. She and her husband, a retired civil servant, had been careful in the way they lived. They had planned their retirement meticulously, especially with regard to their finances. They had a small house with very little garden, and had budgeted so that they could have four holidays abroad every year. I would receive postcards from all corners of the earth: Antigua, Yugoslavia,

Brazil, Florida – they were completely meticulous in their postcarding, too.

Every time they returned from their holiday Mrs Tomlinson came to see me.

'Terrible men in Ecuador,' she would say. 'There I was, trying to sunbathe in a quiet spot. They just wouldn't leave me alone. Chased me all the way back to the hotel.'

The story was repeated in Fiji, New Zealand, Australia, the Costa Brava, and although I realised that in areas where women were more or less in purdah men were uninhibited in their approach to the opposite sex, especially tourists, Mrs Tomlinson probably wouldn't have been my first choice.

I would sit with her after each trip, congratulating her on yet another narrow escape, trying to find what magic it was that stirred men of all nations to such a high pitch of emotion. It was only on her last holiday, which was a trans-Saharan one, that I got some information that led me towards the diagnosis of this phenomenon.

'How were things, Mrs T?' I asked.

'Oh,' she said, 'the men were terrible. I was very, very nearly raped on a camel trip. Look, I've brought you some photos.'

There was a picture of some grinning Tuaregs getting on their camels and there was the seventy-eight-year-old Mrs T. mounting hers, clad in a pair of shorts and nothing else. When I say nothing else, she did have sandals on, but otherwise nothing – she was completely topless. I was taken aback by the pictures.

I said, 'You're topless, Mrs T.'

'Of course, Doctor,' she said. 'I always go topless whenever there's a bit of sun about. I'm not ashamed of my body.'

'You mean,' I said, 'that in all these places you visit, as soon as the sun comes out, it's jumpers off?'

'Why, yes, Doctor,' she replied. 'They say the sun's very good for the body. Gives you vitamin A or something.'

I had this sudden image of Mrs Tomlinson sunbathing in little coves all over the world, stripped half naked, being spied on by some lusty shepherd or gigolo who would then creep up towards the reclining body. On studying the photos carefully I realised why, though Mrs Tomlinson was so often nearly raped, there was heavy emphasis on the *nearly*.

*   *   *

Two of my favourite patients whom I saw regularly over a number of years were Jackie Dean, who suffered from most named medical conditions and a few un-named ones and who was virtually bedridden, and Reg Dawkins, who had an obscure muscular disease and, although confined to a wheelchair, was able to drive a car.

Jackie Dean was hunting mad. Following the installation of an electric chair-lift, which enabled her to get up and down stairs with the help of her sister Mary, she would chase the cat up and down this route, trying to re-create the hunting scene. When the novelty of this game wore off, never dismayed, she began to wear a riding hat in bed with a whipper's-in whip in her right hand. She would have a go at mosquitoes, moths . . . anything that came in her range. I suggested that she try and get in the *Guinness Book of Records* as the only person who went hunting from a bed. She laughed, shouted 'Tally ho!' and expertly flicked the thermometer out of my breast pocket with her riding whip. I felt sure that one day I would enter her room and find a pack of hounds and a couple of horses in there.

Reg Dawkins, who lived in a cottage down near the river, was always battling with the authorities for better facilities, and the authorities fluctuated between doing nothing at all, or seemingly doing everything at once.

Having put on weight he was waiting ages for a new wheelchair when, suddenly, two chairs arrived, one for indoors and one for outdoors. The outdoor chair, however, was too big to pass through the door.

'No problem,' said the man from the equipment department. 'I'll soon fix that.'

The next day he was round again and almost before you

could say 'Jack Robinson', he had knocked a hole in the wall below the window making French windows. So Reg now had two chairs and an extra door; in addition, the man fixed the faulty bar on Reg's bathroom hoist, a useful gadget that enabled him to get in and out of the bath.

I once stayed with Reg and his wife Mary when my family was away – I was on call and needed somebody to man the telephone during the night. It was like staying in a five-star hotel. They completely spoiled me: meals in front of the fire, home-made wine, piles of clean towels, more than I could use in a week. They even offered to bath me by lowering me with the electric hoist; this I politely declined.

Jackie Dean and the Dawkins made great successes of their lives. None of us can do more than fill our days industriously, adventurously and looking out for others. In my early days in practice I had an old lady patient who led a successful life, although she had been bedridden for forty-seven years. Similarly Jackie Dean and the Dawkins lived fully in circumstances that had physical limitations but no limitations on courage, adventure, effort and fulfilment.

CHAPTER 6

Maggots Galore

My advice to patients suffering from stress – to get away for forty-eight hours to a place they'd never been to before – usually worked in helping them to get their problems in perspective. On their return, I sometimes advised the men to take up fishing as part of the longer-term therapy.

It was usually met by the stock objections: 'I'd never have the patience . . .'; 'Don't know the first thing about it . . .'; 'Haven't got any tackle . . .'; 'Can't spare the time . . .'; Don't see the sense . . .'

'Just try it,' I'd say. 'And the fewer fish you catch, the better – only don't tell John Denton that: he'd skin me alive.'

John Denton was the water bailiff on the River Tad, a Mancunian who had opted for the country life to pursue his passion for fishing. He was big, bluff and fond of his ale, with a forthright manner and blunt northern speech that didn't endear him to everybody in Tadchester. But underneath it all he was a big softie and always ready with advice and practical help on fishing. With youngsters he was especially good, and he gave free coaching lessons to the junior section of Tadchester's Anglers' Club.

The juniors owed many of their recruits to John's methods

with juvenile poachers. After discovering that some of the kids he nabbed on the river could not afford tickets because their parents were among the growing number of unemployed in the area, he'd send them along for enrolment to the Tadchester Anglers' Club secretary.

'Say bailiff Denton sent you,' he'd tell the youngsters – after first giving them a dressing-down that frightened the life out of them – 'and don't worry about the membership fee for the first year. That'll be taken care of.'

And so it was, out of John's own pocket, though he did not like that to be known. 'People'd think I was goin' soft or summat,' he'd growl into his pint pot at the Tadchester Arms. 'But I've not forgotten what it was like when me dad was out of work before the war. Wasn't funny, that.'

John combed the jumble sales, and had contacts among auction room staff, ever on the lookout for fishing tackle going cheap. He'd repair any broken gear and take it along to the club to loan to youngsters short of the necessary. Special bits of tackle he would donate as prizes in the junior competition, and devised enough awards to make sure that practically everybody won something.

It was to John that I sent my adult patients for their introduction to angling. He'd kit them out and spend a morning with them on the river. The combination of the right tackle, right bait and John's expertise – and the fact that given enough notice, he would pre-bait the swim the night before to attract the fish – meant that almost everyone caught something on their first outing.

At the stroke of twelve on the town hall clock, John would announce: 'That's it, lad. Twelve o'clock and they stop biting. Pack it in now while you're winning and you won't be disappointed.'

The fish often did stop biting around noon, though sometimes they'd carry on feeding quite happily. But one o'clock was time for John's lunchtime ale in the Tadchester Arms. Twelve o'clock gave him plenty of time to pack up and get there, and to allow him to give in gracefully to the pleas of

'Aw . . . just one more?' A few sneaky tricks known to John alone made sure that there would be just one more, but never two.

'Told you,' John would say as 12.25 approached. 'That's yer lot. Never mind – there'll be other times. Er . . . fancy a pint?'

With a rosy glow that didn't owe everything to the morning in the open air, the novice angler would lurch happily from the Tadchester Arms at 2.35, completely hooked on fishing and all that went with it. Another case of stress was on its way to a cure; another potential depression avoided; another small drain on the health service resources removed, and another member enrolled on Tadchester Anglers' books.

* * *

No matter how many times I went fishing with John, I could never get used to handling maggots, either singly for the hook, or in handfuls as groundbait to attract the fish. It was partly the reaction to the discipline of medical hygiene, but also the fact that a mass of writhing bluebottle maggots looked like an eruption from the primeval slime. Not a pretty sight.

Their size, too, never failed to surprise me. Bait maggots were much bigger than the bluebottle maggots I'd seen on dead creatures in the wild; bigger even than those on corpses I'd had to inspect *in situ* after the discovery of a dead tramp or a suicide in the local woods. I'd never bought maggots at the local tackle shops, either: John always had plenty stacked in an old fridge in his garage and had told me to help myself whenever I was out on the river. Whoppers, they were, every one.

'Wonderful maggots, these, John,' I said one evening at his home, picking out the equivalent of an Olympic weightlifter from his latest batch. 'Do you breed them yourself?'

'No need,' said John. 'I raise my own gozzers on pigeons, and now and again some special butter-fed jobs, but I get most of what I want from Up-the-Hill. Don't even have to collect 'em; there's a few gallons dropped off at my door every Friday.'

'Up-the-Hill? John, you're kidding. I know that times aren't too good up there, but surely they're not breeding maggots to make ends meet?'

'Correction,' said John. '*Over*-the-Hill. T'other side. You've never been to Bleasby's maggot farm? Never heard of "Bleasby's Blockbusters – the Biggest and the Best"? You've led a sheltered life, lad. If you haven't been to Bleasby's, you haven't lived. We'll go there tomorrow.'

'But . . .'

'When's your day off this week?'

'Tomorrow.'

'So no buts. We'll go there tomorrow. Pick you up at nine. Come just as you are.'

John picked me up at nine. Just as I was, which was dressed in my scruffy old fishing clothes after a hasty change and a hastier breakfast. I didn't have the heart to tell John that I'd been out on an emergency call since five that morning.

'Right?' asked John.

'Right,' I yawned.

'Oh, give over,' said John. 'It's not as bad as that. I promise you that you won't be bored. I can tell you've had your breakfast by the marmalade on your top lip, so you've no excuse.'

I followed the intrepid Denton to his Land-Rover, and off we set.

The area over the hill was foreign to me. It was a bleak, windblown stretch of moorland with not a house for miles. Few tourists visited it: it had a desolate *Wuthering Heights* atmosphere about it that was quite depressing. The fact that the few people who did live on the moor were in the catchment area of another practice meant that I did not even know them as patients.

'By heck, John,' I said, as the sturdy Land-Rover was buffeted and rocked by the winds which cut across the moor, 'it's a bit breezy out there.'

'Make the most of it, Bob,' said John. 'There's not much fresh air where we're going . . .'

John drew up outside a solitary bungalow and rang the bell.

He was answered by a pleasant-faced lady in a mob-cap, holding a duster, who turned out to be Mrs Bert Bleasby.

'Morning, John,' I heard her say. 'Bert's over at the farm.'

Declining with thanks the offer of a cup of tea, John strode back to the vehicle. 'Oh, John!' called Mrs Bert after him. 'Just be careful of the dog!'

'So they don't live on the farm, then?' I asked.

'It's not the sort of farm you live on,' chuckled John.

'And what was that about a dog?'

'Dunno,' said John. 'They did have an Alsatian pup a few months back, but she can't mean that. Soft as putty, it was.'

After a five-minute drive, John turned off the road and up a bumpy stone track which led through a screen of stunted trees. Past the trees lay a huddle of low buildings – 'Used to be a pig farm,' explained John – surrounded by a barbed wire fence. There was a sharp whiff in the air, vaguely reminiscent of old stables, which I couldn't quite place.

John opened a gate in the fence and led the way through. Suddenly there was a savage and furious barking and a huge crossbred Alsatian came rushing straight for us. I closed my eyes, covered my vitals, and waited to be dismembered.

'Down, Daffy! DOWN!' roared a voice, and the barking stopped. I opened my eyes to find the dog sitting in front of me, growling menacingly but wagging its tail. A man in a white coat and wellingtons was clumping towards us.

'Oh, it's you, is it?' he greeted John. 'Might have known. How are yer, y'old bugger?'

'All right, till the Hound of the Bleasbyvilles frightened the bloody life out of me,' said John. 'Oh, this is my friend, Dr Clifford. He's fascinated by maggots and I thought you wouldn't mind showing him around.'

'Glad to,' said the man, drawing off a slimy rubber glove, and sticking out his hand. 'Bert Bleasby. Pleased to meet you.'

Bert shook hands with the pair of us and then said, 'Just one thing before we go in. Daffy here had better be introduced. Once he knows you're OK, you've got nothing to worry about. Friends, boy. Friends! Shake a paw.'

The Alsatian, by now thumping its tail frenetically on the ground and slobbering over an enormous tongue, raised its right paw to John and myself in turn. We shook it solemnly. Much better to be a friend of this thing than an enemy. I couldn't work out what its mother had been crossed with – possibly the Creature from the Black Lagoon – but it was certainly bigger than the average Alsatian. There was a hint of soppiness in the eyes, too, which indicated that it was either better-natured than it first appeared or was suffering from repressed schizophrenia.

'Right,' said Bert, leading the way to a little wooden office, 'Let's get you kitted out.'

He gave John and myself a lightweight anorak, a pair of overtrousers and a beekeeper's fine-mesh hood apiece, and picked up a hood for himself.

'What's this for?' I asked, as I put the hood over my head.

'I can tell there are no flies on you, Doctor,' said Bert. 'And I want to keep it that way.'

We went into the nearest building, through a double set of doors.

'Airlocks,' explained Bert as we walked through the first pair. As they closed behind us there was a hissing sound and a fine spray misted the air above us. 'Fly killer,' said Bert. 'Takes care of any bottles who try to run for it.'

Inside the building was a scrubbed concrete area, with several sets of large trays stacked in the corner, and then a door set in a whitewashed breeze-block wall. We walked through this door into another airlock, and again there was the hissing of an automatic fly-killer dispenser.

'This is it, Bob,' said John, as Bert pushed open the second door. 'Be prepared.'

I didn't know what I was supposed to be prepared for, but even if I had, I'd never have believed it. We stepped into a huge room, thirty feet square or more, lit by dazzling neon lights. The air was hot and humid, and buzzing with thousands of black specks. The smell – a weird compound of old dustbins and neglected abattoirs – was revolting. The

38

floor and walls were black . . . and, on closer inspection, *moving*. The noise of several million feeding and breeding bluebottles filled the air like a massed choir of buzz-saws and dentists' drills.

'Don't panic, Bob,' said John as he saw me flinch. 'Bert's never lost a visitor yet. Well, not many . . .'

'This,' announced Bert proudly, 'is the fly room. Honeymoon Hotel for these little beauties.'

As the 'little beauties' crawled all over me, buzzing loudly in my ears through the gauze of the hood, Bert led the way to a series of racks, stacked one above the other.

'Brown sugar,' he said, batting at the black surface which rose with a protesting cloud to reveal the glistening demerara underneath. 'Their wedding breakfast.'

'How very . . .'

'And here,' Bert continued, doing the same to the rack underneath, 'is their nuptial couch.'

I've seen some sights in my time, but at this I nearly threw up. The black cloud rose to reveal chicken heads – hundreds of them – over which the bluebottles were crawling and laying tiny white clusters of eggs.

'Sorry about that,' said Bert, as he noticed me stifle a retch. 'You being a doctor, and that, I thought you'd appreciate these. In the other fly rooms we're starting them off on fish, but that doesn't have the same impact for visitors. Not so spectacular, if you follow my meaning.'

'Please don't apologise,' I muttered, trying not to breathe in. 'This is . . . this is . . . er . . .'

'I agree,' said Bert. 'Fascinating, isn't it?'

As we left the fly room and walked over to another building, Bert explained the system. A constant temperature of 72°F and controlled humidity kept the bluebottles in breeding fettle. When the bluebottles' brief courtship was over, the chicken heads with their clusters of eggs were removed to the hatching bays in the next building; just a few of them being reserved for the next lot of breeding stock.

Then the bluebottles were killed off by spraying with

insecticide – a bit drastic, but no doubt they died happy – and the whole room cleaned down with a high-pressure steam hose. 'When we've finished cleaning, you could eat your breakfast off the floor,' said Bert. I didn't doubt him, but I was glad I'd had breakfast before I came.

'You can take your hoods off now, lads,' said Bert as we walked into the next building. 'You'll find no flies in here.'

Whoof! I now recognised the smell I'd first noticed outside – ammonia. Except that in here it was a thousand times stronger, sending me into a coughing fit and bringing tears streaming down my cheeks.

'Does pong a bit,' said Bert, happily. 'But don't worry, it'll clear your tubes. The county health inspector's over here regularly to check the ammonia levels. And I've got a chemical air-cleaning system that not only changes the air every ten minutes, but neutralises the ammonia before it gets outside. The neighbours would have nothing to complain about, even if we had any.'

The new building we were in was vast, and the floor was divided into dozens of concrete pens, each about eighteen inches deep. Pens at one end had been cleaned out to await the next batch of infant maggots from the hatchery, where heated hatching bays had the maggots wriggling out from the eggs within six hours of laying in the fly room.

But the rest of the pens in here were filled almost to the top with a writhing, wriggling and ammonia-smelling mass of maggots, all feeding heartily on pulverised . . . pulverised *what*?

'You name it,' said Bert. 'Fish, horses, pig, poultry, offal . . . all good stuff. We don't just chuck it in, mind. It takes maggots about six days to reach full size, and during that time they shed their skins about seven times. As soon as they shed, they're ravenous, and that's the time to give 'em the fresh grub. It's like a five-star hotel here: they get a different mix for every feed to build them up quickly. We can't have them just lying around, eating me out of house and home . . .'

I watched the mature maggots being shovelled out of the

end pens and into a huge cleaning machine which riddled them through sawdust to leave them shining bright and free from smell. The cleaned maggots were dumped into a trough about fifteen feet long and easily three feet deep, in which they wriggled and heaved in their millions, waiting to be packed and refrigerated for transport by the lorryload to the big cities and even abroad.

Bert ran his hands through the writhing mass, lifting up a double handful of maggots and trickling them lovingly through his fingers. 'Little beauties,' he breathed. 'Just look at 'em: Bleasby's Blockbusters – the Biggest and the Best!'

Several of the farm's workers hailed Bert as they passed with barrowloads of maggot food, minced and unidentifiable.

'They seem a cheery lot,' I remarked.

'They love it,' said Bert. 'Gets in your blood, maggot-breeding.'

'Where do they get all that stuff from?'

'The cold room,' said Bert. 'Next stop . . .'

As Bert led us into the cold room, I made a mental note to stop asking questions. Around the walls of the room stood thirty or so bins, full of offal. The rest of the place was stacked with frozen corpses: horses, ponies, pigs, poultry, fish, a couple of old milch-cows and – most gruesome of all – crates

41

containing stiff and cold dogs and cats, strayed or old, and put down at local animal homes.

Next to the cold room was the defrosting room, again littered with corpses. These were being dismembered with a chainsaw by a cheerful lad of about seventeen, and fed into a gigantic crushing and mincing machine.

'Look at that,' said Bert proudly, as a former horse poured out of the machine, transformed into a glittering torrent of mince. 'Prime stuff, that. I could eat it myself.'

It was now time to go. I couldn't say that I was sorry, but it was pure squeamishness on my part. Bert was running an efficient, clean and profitable farm, the produce of which gave pleasure to thousands of anglers and employment to locals who were obviously happy in their work, and there was certainly no distress evident among the millions of wriggling maggots, battery-farmed though they were.

'Thanks very much indeed,' I said to Bert as we left. 'It's certainly been an unforgettable experience. But one thing still puzzles me – why have you got barbed wire all around the place? Surely you're not expecting burglars?'

'Expecting 'em?' said Bert. 'We've *had* 'em! With a place as remote as this it's easy for a bunch of cowboys to drive up with a truckful of bins, shovel the maggies in and drive off. There's money in maggots. The blokes who broke in here must have made a tidy sum. That's the reason for the barbed wire – and for Daffy.'

'I knew there must have been a reason for Daffy.'

'Yes. Guard dog, he is. I don't envy the bloke who runs into him on a dark night. Trained him myself. Watch.'

He called Daffy, who'd been wandering around us, slobbering happily. 'Heel, boy!' he commanded. Daffy carried on wandering.

John started to smirk, but soon stopped when Bert handed him a sack. 'Wrap this sack around your arm, John,' said Bert. 'I'll show you.' A bit apprehensively, John wrapped the sack around his right arm.

'Daffy!' commanded Bert. 'Get 'im!'

With a short run and a ferocious burst of barking, Daffy leapt. Teeth closed sickeningly over forearm – and poor old Bert was pulled to the ground and dragged along by the growling dog.

'Geroff, yer daft bugger!' he shouted, cuffing with his free hand. 'Not *me*, you fool!'

John grabbed the dog's collar with his left arm and bashed its nose with his sack-covered right. Eventually the thing cottoned on, let go of Bert and sank its teeth into the sack.

'By 'eck, Bert!' exclaimed John, clouting the dog around the ears until it let go of the sacking and ran off whimpering. 'He's a devil when he's roused.'

'He'll be fine,' panted Bert, 'once he's tasted blood.'

'You're dead right,' said John. 'Just make sure it's not yours.'

We made our farewells to Bert, and to Daffy who came creeping back to distribute slobbering and repentant kisses over one and all, and set off back over the moor with a couple of gallons of complimentary maggots stowed under the seats.

'Nice man, Bert,' I said.

'Lovely feller,' said John. 'But don't let him fool you: he's a very shrewd businessman. Makes a fortune out of that place. Works for it, mind you. Seven-day week for forty-eight weeks in the year, then a month's holiday in the Bahamas for him and his missus. He's done it by running his farm properly and selling quality. I'd never begrudge a man like that.'

'Nor me,' I said. 'Feel a bit sorry for Daffy, though. He's obviously not the dog for the job.'

'Of course he's not,' said John. 'And after today I think Bert will get a proper guard dog firm in and take Daffy back where he belongs – to the bungalow, where he can look after Mrs Bert and frighten the odd rabbit out on the moor.

'Bert's a hard man in business, and an ace with maggots, but he's got a soft spot that any dog can recognise – even one as lunatic as Daffy. Every man to his own trade, I always say.'

As the Land-Rover bumped and lurched through the buffeting winds over the moor top, and with the sting of

43

ammonia still in my nostrils, I realised that I would not have swapped my five a.m. emergency call for a day's more predictable work at the maggot farm, not even if there was a month in the Bahamas at the year's end.

'Dead right, John,' I said. 'Every man to his own trade . . .'

CHAPTER 7

C.P.

For three generations the Wilder family had owned the *Tadchester Gazette*, first published in about 1850. Although their name was prominently displayed at the head of the paper, the Editor of the *Gazette*, the man who *was* the *Gazette*, was Chris Parfitt, generally known in the town as C.P.

C.P. had had some years in Fleet Street and in publishing before coming down to Tadchester, was wise beyond his years and was one of the great local characters. If you worked for the *Tadchester Gazette*, not only had you to meet your deadlines and send in good copy, you had to have the added qualification of being able to drink at least four pints of beer every lunchtime.

'Any good working journalist,' said C.P., 'needs to oil the machinery.'

I always enjoyed C.P.'s company. He had a kind of canny wisdom and you'd find him any lunchtime in the Tadchester Arms with his pipe and a pint. He and his wife, Joyce, would often come and have a meal with Pam and myself. He wrote beautifully. He was far too good for the literary situation that he was in, but he liked the place: he was a keen fisherman and, being virtually a one-man band, he was able to express his own ideas.

I didn't know what part the Wilders played in the *Gazette*'s affairs, other than to accept any profit that C.P. made for them during the year. C.P. was a first-class journalist, a first-class writer, a great character – one of the old school.

He came to see me one day with a lump in his neck that bothered him. I saw him a few times until it began to bother me. It looked like a gland that was just slightly bigger than it should have been, so I got Henry to look at him. We did the usual blood counts and chest X-rays, all the normal checks.

'Better have it out,' advised Henry. 'That shouldn't be much trouble. Really an ENT job though. Not my or Ron Dickinson's field. You'd better go and have it out in Winchcombe.'

I knew the ear, nose and throat surgeon in Winchcombe well and I asked if, as a favour, he would operate on this friend of mine. So, within a couple of weeks, C.P. was in.

The lump took much more digging out than they had expected, though it proved to be harmless, some sort of old tuberculous gland. The ENT surgeon commented that there was a tiny nerve running through the gland which he had to cut through to remove the gland, but he didn't think it was one of any significance.

C.P. was home a couple of days afterwards, very hoarse from the anaesthetic, but otherwise quite well. I reassured him that his voice would come back in a day or two and that a good pint of beer could well lubricate his vocal cords.

However, his voice didn't come back in a day or two. When it hadn't come back in a week or two, he went back to Winchcombe to be seen by the ENT surgeon. The little nerve that he had had to cut through, not that he had any alternative, wasn't a nerve of no significance: it was the recurrent laryngeal nerve. Its importance is that it supplies one of the vocal cords: if you cut it, that vocal cord is paralysed and the patient can speak only in the quietest whisper.

C.P. was sent off to a speech therapist, assured by us that things would be much better. He did, for a time, improve marginally but on the phone he was almost unintelligible. It was very difficult to hear what he had to say and this loss of voice was gradually beginning to destroy him.

'It's terrible,' he whispered. 'I can't even order a beer in a pub that I'm not known in. They can't hear a word I say.

'I don't even know if I can keep my job. Whenever I ring anybody else, particularly in London, they think I'm a heavy breather. I rang a company in Belfast and they set the alarm bells ringing – they thought I was the IRA.'

I encouraged him to persevere with his speech therapy, but little progress was made and C.P. got more and more depressed.

'Can't blame the surgeon,' he whispered. 'He did what he had to do. The lump might have been malignant. Better out than in.'

I knew of nothing more that could be done, and C.P. whispered around the town for almost three years. People, impatient, often turned away before he had made himself understood. Not being able to express himself properly seemed to cut him down. Without the voice, he even shrank physically.

'Until you've lost it, you don't realise how much your voice keeps you afloat in society, protects you from other people,' he wheezed one night in the Tadchester Arms. 'Every minute of the day we're engaged in verbal fencing. By the tone or the volume of your voice, people know how far they can push their luck. And when you've neither tone nor volume the buggers come straight in for the kill.

'Whether it's arguing politics or who was first at the bar, few people have any scruples about shouting you down. Verbal violence. I'd never realised how widespread it is. It's probably saved mankind from a lot of physical violence, but it's not funny when you're in a verbal punch-up with no defence.'

'Aren't you taking all this a bit too seriously?' I asked.

'People knew you when you had a voice. You've not really changed. They know what you're trying to say.'

'There's a big difference,' he said. 'Now they don't have to listen. And a lot of them think that if you can't speak properly, you can't be all there.'

'Not in this day and age, surely?'

'You try it, Bob. Try standing there in the street with the wife, meeting a couple you've known for twenty-odd years. And listen to them saying, "My, he's looking well. Getting over it, is he? That's good." And one of them turns to you and says very slowly and very loudly, "I believe you're doing very well. Yes . . . VERY WELL. Getting over it now, are you?"'

'Then you either give a silly grin, nod politely and say nothing, or you lose your temper. You wheeze away for a bit until you've got your wind up and say, "Of course I'm getting over it, you silly old bugger! But I'm not deaf and daft as well!" '

That was another thing that worried C.P.: losing his temper. With one vocal cord paralysed, it was difficult to regulate the amount of air he took in and breathed out. When he breathed too much out, panic would set in and he would gulp in air to compensate for it. This resulted in hyperventilation and the consequential overdose of oxygen, combined with the adrenalin released by the panic, produced alarming outbursts of bad temper.

'Terrifying Bob,' he said. 'I become completely irrational at times like that. Fight anybody. Bloody silly at my time of life.'

Eventually the speech therapy helped him to control the hyperventilation, and both his temper and voice improved a little. It wasn't enough, however, for someone whose livelihood depended on communication.

He came to see me in the surgery almost exactly three years after his operation. 'I'm off to Liverpool tomorrow,' he whispered, 'to have something done about my throat.'

'That's fine, Chris,' I said. 'But I don't know what *can* be done. What's all this about?

'There's a new technique where they inject liquid Teflon into the paralysed vocal cord. It makes it swell up and brings it back to the middle again, so that the active vocal cord can meet it. That stops all the air escaping and gives you some sort of voice back.'

Most people think of the vocal cords as being like two strings on a guitar, vibrating when air from the lungs is forced through them. But they're more like a split dustbin lid; both halves coming together to make the noise that, with help from the tongue and palate, we take for granted as speech.

But the Teflon injection sounded too good to be true. I checked up with my ENT colleagues. Yes, they said, there was indeed such an operation, a very successful one, but it hadn't yet reached our part of the world. Liverpool was the main centre, where a brilliant ENT surgeon was pioneering the technique.

I felt bad that C.P., rather than me, had found out about the Teflon operation. But it was a very new technique which had originated in the United States as a spin-off, of all things, from research into the use of Teflon as a coating in the space programme.

'See you soon,' said C.P. 'With a pair of non-stick vocal cords.'

'Best of luck, old lad,' I said. 'How are you getting to Liverpool?'

'Driving up,' he said. 'I can't waste time messing around with trains.'

'And how are you getting back?'

'Driving,' he said.

C.P. was certainly getting his confidence back; he was one of the worst drivers I've ever known.

He went off one Tuesday to Liverpool. On the following Friday evening I had a phone call from a voice that I knew but could not place.

'Who's that?'

'It's me,' said the voice.

'Who's me?'

'You've got a short memory. Me. C.P.'

'My God!' I said. 'It's you!'

So it was. C.P. with his voice back – not quite the same, slightly huskier than it used to be, but a firm, clear resonant speaking voice that you could hear perfectly well.

'I don't believe this,' I said. 'What happened?'

'It wasn't the jolliest time I've ever had,' he said. 'They stick a long, fine needle down your throat, into the paralysed vocal cord, and inject the Teflon into it. Every so often you have to say, "Ah", so that they can judge when enough has been pumped in.'

'So it's done under local anaesthetic?' I asked.

'The local anaesthetic is given from the *inside*, so you finish up with a throatful of needles. It's known in the trade as an uncomfortable process, which is the understatement of the century. The Teflon injection itself should last a lifetime, but I'd have it done once a year if I had to. That surgeon's a bloody saint.'

Certainly the operation seemed like a miracle. After talking in a whisper for three years, suddenly C.P. could speak again quite normally. This was medicine at its very best; no drama or heroics, but a delicate and simple procedure performed by

the best and most skilful hands. And it couldn't have happened to a nicer chap.

In spite of C.P.'s confidence, I wondered if the improvement would last or whether it was just temporary. But it did last. Five years later, he was still chatting away quite normally, as are others who have had the same operation, which is now much more widely established.

The cutting of that particular nerve sometimes happens when the thyroid gland is operated on. These days, the few who are unable to speak – and even those unable to speak for many years – can be given back their voices in less than an hour on the operating table.

One of C.P.'s problems was in adjusting to the volume of his new voice.

'I keep forgetting that I don't have to force it any more,' he said one lunchtime in the Tadchester Arms. 'Sometimes I build myself up to make myself heard, suddenly find I'm shouting, and get accused of being aggressive. People who were only too ready to shout me down when I had no voice, now back off and sulk in corners. You really can't win.'

As C.P. left the pub I was joined by John Denton, who was also enjoying a liquid luncheon in the Tadchester Arms.

'I know what he means,' said John. 'I've seen it happen in my own chicken run.'

'What? C.P. in your chicken run?'

'No, you silly bugger. There was this damn great rook once that used to march straight into my henhouse every day and pinch the eggs. Cocky, aggressive, bold as brass, and making threatening noises that had all the hens running for cover.

'One day I'd had enough, and I gave it one from my twelve-bore as it was coming in to land. I only winged it and the thing ran into the henhouse to hide. That was its first mistake . . . and its last.

'When I got in there, it wasn't the proud, arrogant, nest-robbing rook any longer. It was a disabled, vulnerable beast, and all the hens were fighting to get at it, pecking it to death.'

'What's that got to do with C.P.?'

'Only that he's fine now he can use himself again. But there were a few in this pub who didn't hesitate to pile in and peck him when he couldn't peck back. Makes me feel ashamed of myself.'

'Why? You didn't peck him, surely?'

'Yes, I did.'

'And when was that?'

'Five years ago. Just before the operation to get his voice back. When he lost his temper and played hell with me.'

'What for?'

'Shooting that bloody rook.'

CHAPTER 8

Singing for Supper

In between surgery hours I was still plugging away at my writing and had had some small success. I had one brief moment of glory when the *Sunday Express* serialised a humorous book. It was all very exiting. The first instalment was published the Sunday we were returning from a holiday in France and there were copies of the *Sunday Express* being read all over the boat. There were none left in the shop. I was dying to rush up to somebody and say, 'By the way, I wrote the serial.'

Eventually one rather nice lady who we were sitting next to in the cafeteria put hers down and I said, 'Would you mind if I borrowed this for a moment?', and there was my story.

The serialisation brought an approach from a famous lecture agency. I would be in great demand as a speaker, they said. Their list of speakers included leading figures in the land: sportsmen, politicians and authors. I felt extremely flattered, and I'd always fancied myself as an after-dinner speaker. I looked forward to a change in my economic circumstances, thinking how much money I would make, and imagining myself at livery dinners and such, having Lord Mayors and Royalty rolling in the aisles.

I waited expectantly. I had been on the agency's books for two years before I had my first request, which was to speak at a luncheon of food manufacturers next day in London. London, by the next day, was quite impossible.

Six months later were was another request, the possibility of speaking to some library staff in Nottingham. They eventually decided they didn't want me.

Then after three years, success. I was asked to go and speak to the Round Table of a small Lancashire town. I was to receive travelling expenses, plus overnight hotel accommodation and a fee of £150. It sounded too good to be true.

It so happened that I had two lady patients who were born in this town and they filled me in with a lot of background information. I had some difficulty in placing it on the map but eventually found it was on the Yorkshire–Lancashire border, nearer to Manchester than it was to Leeds.

I accepted this invitation, which of course I thought would be the first of many, realising that I would cost the organisers in the region of £230. As I had been a Round Tabler in the past, I was surprised that somebody was going to pay that much for me to speak to them. I imagined that they must all be very keen writers and want to know something about writing.

The agency said the lecture should last threequarters of an hour and I set about preparing it.

I received travel instructions: I was to report to the King's Hotel, where I was to stay, and then to dinner at the Black Stag. Before I left, I rang the organiser to check on the length of my speech. He said, 'Oh no, not forty-five minutes, just your usual. An after-dinner speech – about twenty minutes.' This I knew I could do standing on my head. I could already see them being convulsed in laughter but it sounded a lot of money for me to be paid to go all this way to Lancashire. Although this town featured very largely in the eyes of two of my lady patients, it didn't seem to feature very largely in anybody else's.

I travelled up to Lancashire via London, Leeds and a

branch line going out to Bradford, doubling back through the Calder Valley, following a little river bed. Wherever there was water, there was a mill. We were going through a deep valley with splendid hills reaching up either side.

I said to a travelling companion, 'Excuse me, are these the Yorkshire Dales?'

'Not these,' he said. 'These are bugger all,' and that really set the tone for the rest of my day.

All of my trains were late. One of them broke down. And on my way up the branch line we were standing, packed solid in the carriage.

I arrived at the small station to find that my speaking engagement was in a pleasant little town, nestling at the foot of the surrounding hills. It had a splendid town hall, out of all proportion to the size of the place, and I was told by several people that it was much bigger than Halifax. There didn't appear to be too many places of entertainment: there was a Coffee Club, which closed at 4.30, which was new and obviously the social gathering point of the people; and Tom's Tea Bar, which was a little further down the social scale. The town looked a bit run down and, looking back through population figures, I found that the number had actually halved over the last twenty years.

The hotel was clean, comfortable, and I was the only guest. No one came to meet me, although I understood that they had rung to see if I had arrived, and at the appropriate time I made my way to the Black Stag.

I was greeted by the chairman of the local Round Table who fetched me a drink and introduced me to a puzzled vice chairman who said, 'Where did they get you from?' I was surrounded by a lot of happy, hearty, enthusiastically drinking young men, who didn't seem too interested in me. My earlier, unpaid, speaking engagements had been at places like Women's Institutes, where I was fêted as the guest of honour, and a couple of literary lunches where I had been made a real fuss of. But here I was a professional performer.

Most of the assembled company, ninety in all, were well

liquored before we went upstairs to a packed dining room where there was lively discussion with excellent food and good wine. The man on my right said, 'I'm nervous about you.' He questioned me closely on how I had been booked and what I was going to do. At this stage, I was beginning to wonder also.

Picking up the programme, I saw that it was the twenty-fifth anniversary of this Round Table and I was to give a speech in reply, on behalf of the guests. £230 seemed an awful lot of money for that.

The dinner dragged on and on. At about 9.45 the first speaker – and there were three to precede me – rose. I thought all three speeches would be short and sweet, as the audience was waiting for this famous doctor-writer-broadcaster. Just as the first speaker started, the door burst open and in came a crowd of boisterous, half-dressed ladies. Some were made up as French waitresses and some dressed as French male painters with burnt cork moustaches. They were the 'better halves' of the assembled males, determined not to miss out on their husbands' night out. There was a distinct chill about their arrival but once there, they wouldn't go away. There was a tremendous uproar with shouts of 'Get 'em off. Take 'em down!' One or two were mauled by some of the diners who were now fairly well in their cups.

Eventually, after twenty-five minutes, the girls' leader managed to deliver her speech, which was to present the Chairman of the Round Table with a leather briefcase which he had to open. Inside was a present . . . a pair of knickers – what else? – and the room again resounded with shouts of, 'Get 'em off! Get 'em off!'

Eventually the girls dispersed and the first speaker, the original founder of this particular Round Table, began his speech again. It was very witty and much appreciated, very local in content – when Jack did this and George did that, and when Herbert and Dick did so and so – and he had them in fits of laughter about parochial things and parochial events. His promised 'few words' lasted for threequarters of an hour, but he was very funny.

Meanwhile the rest of the ninety guests were getting steadily more stoned.

The next speaker was a veterinary surgeon, the Area Chairman of the Round Table, who was both poorly sighted and hard of hearing. His hearing aid was in his glasses and when he took his glasses off he could neither see nor hear. This was pointed out to him in very explicit language by the inebriated members of the various Round Tables present. He spoke for only half an hour, again very local stuff, being rude about the people who were stoned and dropping the tone steadily.

By the time he finished it was eleven o'clock and there was a ten-minute break. The ten-minute break stretched until 11.15, when it was the turn of the Chairman of the Round Table to speak.

He was a very pleasant chap who had done his best to hold the evening together. He had a French wife, which explained the attire of the ladies who had burst in upon us. Whilst Chairman of this particular Round Table he had apparently committed the heinous crime of spending a five-week holiday in France that necessitated his missing two Table meetings. During his speech the assembled company spent most of its time boisterously pointing out his French connection and neglected duties.

His speech began by mentioning briefly everyone who was present. I forget what he said about me but it was very little. His main story was about a man on a plane radioing airport control in New York that the pilot had died, the navigator had died, the co-pilot had died and that he – who had never flown before – was manning the aircraft. He told airport control that he was flying at 8,000 feet, and at 700 miles per hour, and upside down.

'Don't worry,' said airport control, 'we'll talk you in. How do you know you're at 8,000 feet?'

'I can see it on the dial,' said the man.

'How do you know you're flying at 700 miles an hour?'

'I can see it on the dial,' said the man.

'And how do you know you're flying upside down?' asked the controller.

'Because of the shit coming out of my collar,' said the man.

This was the joke of the evening. It had the audience in fits. This was the man I had to follow. Eventually, at 12.15, it was my turn to speak. By now those who weren't boisterously drunk had nodded off to sleep. The Master of Ceremonies, who I think had taken a dislike to me, introduced me with some reluctance: perhaps my fee had been debated at some bitter Round Table meeting.

I have used various pseudonyms for my bits of writing and somehow this chap had got hold of all of them and he introduced me by saying, 'Our next speaker, and I've got to read this, reckons he is Dr Robert Andrew, Dr Clifford, Dr Pheasant and, for all I know, Doctor f– – – ing Partridge. I don't know what he's going to talk about but he is going to respond to the guests.'

I got up and did my twenty-minute crowd-basher. It had delighted thousands of Women's Institute meetings, adjustments had made it a wow at literary luncheons and literary dinners, it had held its own on distinguished occasions such as the after-dinner speech to the Association of British Medical Publishers, and even the World Business Council at Gleneagles, but it wasn't right for this Round Table dinner.

There was a bit of polite laughing at the beginning, then automatic laughing, plus a lot of barracking. I sweated through my twenty minutes and when it was over, sat down.

'What about your expenses?' said the Chairman.

'Oh,' I said in a generous moment, 'forget them. I've been a Round Tabler in the past and this is my contribution to the evening.' As my expenses were more than £50 this was indeed generous but I realised that I was going to write this off as an expensive experience.

The man who had worried about me bought me a drink and said, 'That was fine.' The Chairman said, 'That was excellent.' But nobody else said anything.

Two people spoke to me afterwards; one tried to be nice and the other spoke because I looked as though I was lonely. Nobody saw me off and I made my way back to the hotel. I read a book, went to sleep and caught my train back to the Calder Valley.

To my surprise, a few days later, there was a cheque for £150 from the Chairman with a note saying, 'Thank you for your excellent speech and for not claiming expenses. Yours in friendship . . .'

So there I was, at home. I noticed that the cheque wasn't a Round Table cheque but his own personal business account. I hoped the poor man hadn't paid it all himself.

What a sell. It must have cost them £10 a minute for me and nobody had listened. I was glad that initially the agent had written to me saying that she had arranged for them to pay me in cash. I had written back to say that I would find this highly embarrassing; could she make sure that I was paid by cheque? I could just imagine at the end of the meal, with ninety people watching, as they peeled off £230 in notes at the end of my boring twenty-minute interlude. They hadn't really needed a speaker at all. They were extremely nice, they just made a mistake. Still it was a great experience for me. I hope it wasn't too expensive an experience for them.

CHAPTER 9

Recovering My Zip

It must have been a measure of the state of mind I had unknowingly drifted into when, one Sunday morning over a cup of tea in bed, Pam said, 'You are always sending people away for forty-eight hours. Why don't you take your own advice and see if you can get your zip back. Look, here are some organised trips, "City Weekends all over Europe".'

Pam is persuasive, and the idea seemed a good one at the time, so the next day I booked myself a single passage for a weekend in Salzburg.

It was only as the time grew nearer that I had doubts about what I might have let myself in for. As a logical man, I realised that Salzburg – being further east and north – would probably be cold, wet and sloshy. It was not high enough to have the sun that goes with Alpine coldness. I also rationalised that, as it was between-season time, most things would be shut down.

I couldn't visualise what I was going to do on my own, other than drinking, eating and sloshing about in the cold and wet. However, the idea of two days in a luxury hotel appealed to me. Who knows what adventures might lie ahead? Apart from that, I couldn't get my money back.

As a family, and individually, we never ever seem to be able to do anything in an ordinary way. There is always some natural or man-made disaster that dogs us on our travels. Two days before my planned trip, the British Rail overtime ban started. Although many people blamed it on a Communist plot, I knew that the go-slow was directly related to the fact that I wanted to use the railways. However, I worked out that by careful planning I could make a leisurely journey to Austria and back. There was time; I had chosen my weekend in the middle of a ten-day holiday.

I saw from the tour brochure that I had to be at Luton airport at 7.15 a.m. I booked a room at an hotel adjoining the North London Air Terminal, thus ensuring that there would be no last-minute rushes anywhere. All I would have to do would be to get out of bed and get on the bus.

In spite of the go-slow, if I travelled up in the afternoon before, I should have no problems.

Fate did not mean things to be this way. The practice decided to have a party on the eve of my departure, and for every reason I was unable to miss this. So I eventually went to catch my train at 9 p.m. – which of course didn't arrive until 10.30 p.m. – which got me to the hotel at 3.30. To catch my bus I had to be at the Terminal at 6.30 a.m. Being a cautious man, I not only booked a 6 o'clock call with the night porter, but also rang him from my bedroom before falling exhausted into bed. Checking my watch when the alarm call came, I saw that it was 6.25, giving me five minutes to get packed, shaved, washed, dressed and round to the Air Terminal.

I rushed downstairs, half-shaved, half-clothed, dragging my case, and enquired from the night porter on the way out what had happened to his timing mechanism. His reply was brief, and roughly translated, meant, 'Get stuffed!'

This set the pattern for the day. There are some days when one's aura just does not seem to be functioning, and one's dominant personality doesn't fire on all cylinders.

I made the bus in time and got to the airport in time, so it did look as if I was going to get away. By the time the plane was due to fly out, however, the passengers had not been called, and there was mounting anxiety among the group hoping to get to Salzburg.

Eventually we set off, half an hour late, in a pink plane, to arrive at Munich airport in snow and ice. We had a two-hour bus journey to Salzburg ahead, and at this stage I realised that a cold which had begun the day before had really started to stream, and that a boil had begun to erupt on the left side of my nose.

The first news at Munich was that, because of the ice and snow, the bus journey was likely to take three hours, which it did. The autobahn was blocked by an overturned lorry, and the bus had to go along part of the German Alpine route near Berchtesgarten, through Insole, the venue for the world ice speed-skating championships, and eventually arrived at our hotel late in the afternoon.

The hotel was absolutely luxurious. Cultured and gentlemanly diplomats waited on us at the porters' desk. Hordes of waiters, waitresses and page boys buzzed about and hovered around, helpful and smiling. This was the life.

For the evening, there was a choice between a Mozart concert and a folk-dancing display. Being uncultured, I opted for the folk-dancing, and set off with the courier and a British couple to the Sternbrau, resigned to the spectacle of blonde pigtailed maidens and boot-slapping men in leather shorts. We arrived to be told that the folk-dancing was off, but we could stay for a meal.

All through the meal, the loss of personality dominance dogged me. A round of drinks was served to everyone but me. The waiter had forgotten. Everybody was served with the first course. Except me. My first course arrived with the second, so I was able to allow my wiener schnitzel to cool while I ate my hors-d'oeuvre.

Back at the hotel, our party swelled, and I found myself buying a round of seven brandies and one cup of coffee. I had thought the drinks might be expensive, but this was terrifying

– £24 for seven brandies. One glass of brandy cost the same as I'd paid for a bottle on the plane.

The weather in Salzburg was just as I had anticipated, bitterly cold and windy, with driving snow overhead and slush underfoot. An expedition to the shops not only gave me a severe chill on my bald head (I hadn't brought a hat), but turned the taps full-on for my cold and gave my growing boil a boost. I sat in the hotel with a boil on my nose, a streaming cold, having just paid £24 for seven brandies, having had three and a half hours' sleep, travelled several hundred miles, and missed a folk-dancing evening. *This* was the life?

Mercifully, it was time for bed. I fell fast asleep to wake up with a start at quarter to four, aroused by the noise outside. I looked through the window to see people in cars, people window shopping, people bawling cheerily and loudly at each other. Obviously an old Salzburg custom. I slept fitfully for the rest of the night, but determined to make the most of my holiday the next day.

When I woke up, the atrocious weather had deteriorated, my cold was much worse and the boil was much bigger. Everybody had a companion except me, which was not surprising. I did not have a lot to offer.

I made repeated forays against the blizzard, but the shops were so expensive I couldn't afford to buy anything. I could get a cup of coffee, though, for 50p at a coffee shop fifty yards from the hotel. By having coffee once every two and a half hours I managed to keep my interest and spirits up.

The proffered entertainment of the Saturday night was another Mozart concert or a performance of *The White Horse Inn*. *The White Horse Inn* being nearer, I plumped for that. I couldn't drink any more coffee.

My seat cost me £8, and I was in the second row of a half-empty theatre with a cast that seemed to be composed half of fairly good professionals and half of pretty rotten amateurs. Not speaking any German, I couldn't understand a word, but did recognise one or two tunes, and tried not to let my cold interfere with the dialogue. I had to wait until the chorus

broke into song before I blew my nose. One light relief was to see a male ballet dancer obviously rupture himself catching his partner in a flying swan movement. I was glad somebody else wasn't having the luck.

Back to the hotel, and more brandies. Even whisky was £2.50p a glass, so there wasn't much point in changing my brand. I got into conversation with three young German girls, eighteen-year-olds from a domestic-science college. The Deutschmark was so strong that they had come to this palace of luxury to have a cheap weekend. Bully for them. They wanted to talk, and it seemed my luck had changed, but I was buttonholed in the bar by a German bore who wanted to practise his English. It was not until four o'clock in the morning that I was able, bored out of my skull, to stagger away to my couch.

I was woken at 8 o'clock. By now I was pouring catarrh and could hardly open my left eye because of the boil. I was sneezing, I was cold, and I was a long way from home.

It wasn't snowing this morning, thank goodness, and I was able to wander around the town and see some of its beauty. It was indeed beautiful, and would have been even more beautiful if most of it hadn't been closed.

The autobahn was empty on the way back, Sunday driving not being a habit in Germany. A freezing three-hour stop in Munich, my cold getting worse, and back to London to find no trains running, no hotels with vacancies. I finished up sleeping on the floor of a friend's flat for the night, sharing it with the dog, who obviously wasn't as tired as I was.

At Paddington Station next day, I eventually found a train about to move off, and arrived home exhausted, feeling as if I had been to the North Pole.

Pam was all concern: 'Oh, you poor darling! What a terrible boil!'

The children looked at me with less compassion: 'Serve him right. Swinging weekends at his age!'

Before my ten-day holiday was up, by dint of careful nursing and an alcohol-free diet, I was fit enough to stagger back to work. I was welcomed by Gladys and Grace.

'Good God, Doctor Bob!' said Grace. 'You must tell us this magic formula you have for getting fit in forty-eight hours. I have an old uncle I want to finish off. By the look of you, it might just do the trick . . .'

CHAPTER 10

Planning Ahead

One of the conditions Pam made before I went to Salzburg, was that we booked our summer holiday. The only people who were available for this were Paul, Jane, Pam and I, so I booked an apartment in La Tranche, a French seaside resort south of the Sable-d'Olonne.

We love France. Nothing pleases us more than to wander along the secondary roads of France putting up in little hotels in remote villages, shopping in local markets and eating lunch – crisp French bread, a bottle of wine, cheese and pâté – by the nearest river.

We rarely travel beyond the borders of France as there is so much we haven't seen and we cannot think that there can be anything better. When we have strayed into Spain or Italy we have always been glad to get back to France.

We crossed to Cherbourg, our favourite crossing, and ambled through France spending our first night at Vitré which is a beautiful medieval town with more churches per head of population than any I have seen, and a magnificent castle. We then spent a day wandering leisurely along secondary roads with one more night's stop before arriving at La Tranche itself, to find a clean apartment overlooking the beach with good facilities. There were young French people in the apartment upstairs, who took Paul and Jane off to discos, and there was sailing and windsurfing and swimming. A nice-sized town where you could shop, a large market, plenty of boulevard cafés where you could sit in the sun and watch people go by. There wasn't a great deal of entertainment in the evening but it was always pleasant to stroll into the town and have a coffee or a drink and watch the townsfolk drift by.

There were day trips to La Rochelle, marvellous sea-food meals and plenty of muscadet, the wine of the region. It all went too quickly. We had a really splendid holiday – sunshine and sea, good wine and made friends with lots of French people.

Being a superb organiser, I decided we would cut our holiday short. Too often our holidays had been ruined by the mad dash for the boat so I had planned a hard day's driving to find somewhere in Normandy where we could spend two leisurely days unwinding before a short journey to the boat for our return home.

The journey went splendidly. We were exactly halfway up the Cherbourg peninsula at about four o'clock and started, in no hurry at all, to look for decent accommodation.

By nine o'clock and eighty miles further on, we had found nothing. What we hadn't realised was that this was a French public holiday and every single room everywhere had been booked months in advance.

In despair, worn out and exhausted, I said, 'We'll just have to sleep in the car for the night.'

We had seen a sign 'Camping – Agricultural', and as I wasn't going to park in the road we made off in the appropriate direction. The camp consisted of a field with six caravans and a tap.

I enquired of one of the campers where the farm was, so that we could ask permission to sleep there in our car for the night. In my halting French, supplemented by Jane's A-level vocabulary, we explained our position to the farmer. He picked up the telephone directory and rang friend after friend, to see if they could put us up. This was French hospitality at its best. He tried everyone he could think of, but without success.

He sat thinking for a moment, then he said, 'I have an idea.' He had a *gîte*, a letting house which he had rented to a honeymoon couple. It was a large house with three bedrooms and this was the last night of their honeymoon, so he wondered if they would mind sharing it with four bedraggled, tired Anglaises (the *gîte* not the honeymoon) on their last night.

He came back from the phone, smiling and triumphant.

'They will be pleased to have you.'

Pierre and Margaret were absolutely delightful. Perhaps they were a bit bored after seven days on their own in an isolated hamlet. Certainly they went out of their way to be hospitable.

'Not eaten yet?' This horrified them. Ham, eggs, bread, soup, pâté, all appeared. They produced a bottle of wine and I produced a bottle of duty-free gin, a litre, which I had anticipated taking home. This was a new drink to them and they drank it by the tumberful.

'It's very good,' they agreed. 'Now you must try some of our local spirit.' And this was Calvados.

By now we were almost stoned. Even Jane, who doesn't normally drink at all. But yet more wine and more Calvados were consumed. We looked through the wedding photographs, then the bride fetched her wedding dress from upstairs and eventually the bridegroom brought out his wedding suit, all of which received their full share of admiration. Finally, we all tottered to bed.

We woke in the morning to huge, steaming bowls of coffee, croissants, butter and peach jam. Names and addresses were swapped and later on, when we got back to England, we sent them a wedding present. The farmer would take nothing. How kind the French were.

We still had one more night to go in France and the public holiday was still going on so we decided to start looking for an

hotel at eleven o'clock in the morning and found a moderate
one which had its own dining room. We had lost the incentive
to stray too far. All we were thinking of, after the previous
tiring and alcoholic day, was to get home.

For dinner, Pam decided to become adventurous and have
something from the menu, which, from her French translation,
she thought was sweetbreads. She didn't like the taste of them
very much and they looked like nothing I had ever seen
before. In one corner of the dining room I could see a
television buzzing away. There was a news bulletin, something
to do with the ports. I tried to attract the family's attention.

I said, 'I think there's something wrong. They're shutting
the ports or something.'

'Oh, shut up, Dad,' said Paul. 'Just stop worrying. You worry all the time. You're going to spoil our holiday.'

I *was* worried however, and on questioning at the hotel desk, I found there had been some trouble at the ports and there was a possibility of their being blockaded the next day. My heart sank. We all had pressing commitments on our return to England.

We awoke early and turned the car radio on and found that my fears of the night before were confirmed. The French had blockaded all their ports in an industrial dispute. Motorists were advised not to go into the main ports where they might get stuck and were requested to head for Zeebrugge in Belgium where there was a chance that they might be picked up.

Zeebrugge was 380 miles away, a tortuous route across country and through all sorts of industrial towns like Lille. This was the moment that Jane, poring over her French dictionary, chirped up: 'I know what you were eating last night, Mother. It wasn't sweetbreads, it was brains.'

Whether it was just the thought of this – Pam had already been feeling queasy – or whether they were bad I don't know, but Pam was continually sick all the way from Cherbourg to Zeebrugge. I think she must have been sick at least once every half hour for the whole day, far outstripping any effort of Paul's, who up until then had been the family's champion vomiter.

Paul navigated. We sped on, first on motorways and then, on a direction from Paul, we turned right on to mile after mile of cobbled roads through Lille, all of which looked the same to me. The signposting was poor or non-existent and as far as I knew we could have been going round and round in circles.

'Why did we leave the motorway, Paul?' I asked.

'Oh,' he said, 'I thought we'd been on it too long and got a bit scared. I thought we would be better going through a town.'

It was like going through Manchester and Wigan twice, with no signposts.

Eventually we reached Zeebrugge. There was a queue of cars ahead. I had no idea whether it was short or long. The car in front of me pulled out to make an extra lane. I duly pulled out and followed it. I was met by a crowd of screaming, abusive fellow countrymen, accusing me of trying to jump the gun. I had assumed that we were just squaring up to go on the boat, I hadn't realised that there was a queue of cars two miles ahead of us and I had to back shamefacedly, passing about thirty cars, with the children and Pam hiding in their seats, pretending they weren't with me.

Eventually, after much waiting and inching forward, we got on board a huge ferry boat and arrived at Dover at eight in the morning, having had no sleep. With Pam exhausted from her vomiting, me with a sort of ache in my side, we drove back from Dover just in time for me to start the afternoon surgery.

At supper that night Paul said, 'Good idea of yours that, Dad, two resting days before the boat. It certainly settles you down.'

He managed to duck as I swung a punch at his left ear.

The ache in my side persisted. It wasn't a bad ache but it didn't go away. It was not dissimilar to, but not nearly as bad as two episodes I had had in that region before. These attacks had been what is called ureteric colic and meant that a little stone that I had formed in the kidney was passing down the tube that led from the kidney to the bladder. I had had two of these and the pain is absolutely excruciating. The first one I had had during a ward round when I was in Tadchester, the second was when we were at the furthest outpost of a trans-Saharan safari: I was the medical officer to an expedition taking some rich Americans round the Sahara who were not at all comforted by the sight of the expedition doctor writhing on the floor in pain.

Happily, after a few days of really intense pain, the first two stones passed. They say the pain is worse than childbirth. Men say that anyway – I have never met a woman who had had both a renal stone and given birth. Stones and babies have a similarity in presentation in that they come in waves.

You can be perfectly well, then suddenly, out of the blue, you get a great wave of pain going right down one side of your body. You confirm the presence of the stone by having an investigation called an intravenous pyleogram. Some fluid is squirted into your vein, which for a few seconds feels as if you had been filled with hot mustard. This is a dye which can be watched as it goes through your kidneys and it will show whether your kidneys are blocked and whether there are any stones in your kidney, ureter (the tube from the kidney to the bladder), or even in the bladder itself.

My intravenous pyleogram showed a stone halfway down my ureter, three or four times bigger than any stone I had ever seen before. The surprising thing was that it wasn't causing me as much pain as the others.

I went to Winchcombe to see the urologist.

'Well, Bob,' he said. 'Your stone is probably four times bigger than the maximum size that should pass out of the system on its own. It's not stopping the kidney working at present so I think we can afford safely to watch it. It does mean having an X-ray, perhaps every month, and testing your water regularly. If this one gets stuck, I'm afraid it will be at the junction where the ureter meets the bladder. Then I'm afraid you'll need an operation to have it removed. But occasionally big ones will pass, in spite of their size.'

My stone's progress down my ureter was very, very slow indeed. After eighteen months it had reached the end of the ureter and was poised to go through the tiny little valve into the bladder. I went to my urologist.

'I don't think it's going to go any further, Bob,' he said. 'We'll fix an operation for three weeks' time.'

'Can't you sort of reach up and grab it from there?' I said.

'No,' he said, 'it would do too much damage to the valve in the bladder. We'll fix the operation just the same.'

I was depressed by the news of this forthcoming operation and it must have shown in my attitude to the patients at the next morning surgery. One of my regulars, Mrs Cookson, a dark, energetic lady, interrupted my questioning of her by saying, 'There's something wrong, Doctor.'

'Yes,' I said impatiently, 'try and tell me what it is.'

'No,' she said. 'There's something wrong with you. You know I have second sight. For a change, you tell me what is wrong with you.'

One of Mrs Cookson's claims was that she could communicate with the spirits, particularly those with healing powers.

Reluctantly I told her about my forthcoming operation. She listened intently. When I had finished she said, 'Don't worry. I'm in touch with a spirit who's especially good at moving stones. You've been very kind to me in the past, Doctor. I'll see you don't have to have an operation.'

I did politely remind her that only last year she had had an operation to remove gallstones of her own: what was the spirit doing at this time?

'Don't laugh at me, Doctor,' she said. 'I can only get the spirits to work on other people. You just wait and see.'

She got up and determinedly walked out of the consulting room, brows furrowed, quite forgetting that she had not told me the reason for her visit. I got on with the surgery and the rest of the day's work without another thought about Mrs Cookson's offer of spiritual help.

I went home brooding about the impending operation. During the evening surgery that night I had all sorts of funny feelings down below. A bit more pain, a few aches in different places, a great desire to pass water, then, suddenly, I realised the stone was in my bladder. I rang everybody in triumph – no operation, marvellous. No hospitals for me because I knew that anything that got into the bladder could make the last few inches to daylight without trouble.

In fact, this particular stone, because of its size, didn't and it had to have a little help over the last couple of inches. But, no operation.

Could it have been Mrs Cookson's friend who gave my stone a last push? Who knows? Many unexplained things happen in medicine. Big stones like mine do pass sometimes but it was all rather eerie that it should happen the very day that Mrs Cookson said she was going to get to work on me.

The next time I saw her she was completely unsurprised about what had happened.

'I told you so, Doctor,' she said, 'but I can't do this for everybody so don't go round telling people I arranged it for you.'

I just had to leave it at that and I have had to disguise her under a pseudonym, but if she does have the powers she claims, what an asset she would be to any hospital – I think they would have to make her a consultant straight away.

I went with glee to see my urologist, taking my stone in a pot.

'Well done, Bob,' he said. 'It certainly saved you a lot of inconvenience and a major operation.'

'Yes,' I said, 'I didn't think I was meant to be in hospital.'

I was delighted because an operation would have interfered with all my summer activities, boating, seine-net fishing and whatever. I came home delighted to Pam.

'No hospitals or operations, darling,' I said. 'How about that?'

'Oh good. It's amazing how Nature takes care of you,' she said. 'Why not take this as an opportunity to lose a bit of weight and stop smoking. I noticed you have dropped back to puffing the odd pipe and cigar again.'

'Right,' I said, 'I'll become a reformed character. I am definitely going to keep clear of hospitals from now on.'

Three weeks later I had to change my mind.

CHAPTER 11

The Heart of the Matter

I felt in desperate need of a boat. Our last boat had disintegrated and here we were, living down by the river with no form of water transport. A couple of years back I had gone with Pam's father, Gerry, to Wales to explore the possibility of a boat, but it turned out to be a dud. When we had an unexpected and back-dated extra payment from the practice I went straight to the Sheridan Boat Stores. Without consulting anybody, I bought an eight-foot fibre-glass dinghy, a brand new outboard, oars, rowlocks and a fire extinguisher. They had no trolley for me to wheel it down to the river but arranged to have one made, and deliver it as soon as possible. I boarded the dinghy at the Sheridan Boat House and travelled home in it. One of the boatyard engineers came with me to explain the working of the engine and helped me carry the boat up to the house, which was a bit of a struggle. Pam was out at the time so we stowed it in the garage.

When Pam came home I said, 'I've a surprise for you, darling.'

'I know what it is,' she said. 'It's a new fridge.'

'Not quite,' I said, 'but close. Now, how can we live near a river and be boatless? We've bought a new boat.'

I could see her heart sink. I was running true to form. I had surprised her with the first car, not a Mini-Cooper or venerable MG, but a ten-hundredweight van that suited my seine-net fishing expeditions. Now we had a boat instead of a fridge. But she took it well.

'I expect you're right,' she said, 'when can we have a trip in it?'

'We really ought to wait for a trolley,' I said, 'but I think I might manage it on my back.'

'Are you sure?' she said.

'Nothing to it. It's my day off tomorrow; if it's nice, we'll have a trip down river.'

The day dawned bright and clear and I managed somehow to pack the boat on my back. By bending double, nearly kissing my knees, I could balance it and I staggered down the two hundred yards to the river. Then I went back and fetched the engine, which wasn't quite as heavy. Pam brought the petrol tank and oars, and we had a lovely trip. The tide was in, and we sped up to Tadchester Bridge: we could fairly skim along in this little boat. Then back towards the house to be able to land before the tide shot out and left us with yards of mud to wade through.

We took off the engine and various impedimenta. I hitched the boat on my back again and staggered up the hill towards the house. It really was a struggle: it took me every bit of my strength and energy and, because I was bent, it did make the muscles of my chest hurt. I felt it pushed me to my physical limit and my chest continued to ache afterwards. The pain didn't go away until I had sat down for a bit, so I rested before going out again to fetch the engine and other boating paraphernalia.

'Before we go out on the river again,' I said to Pam, 'we'll wait for the trolley.'

I thought I had strained something. My chest was a bit uncomfortable most of the next day and I was on duty that night. Coming back from a call Up-the-Hill, I felt extremely uncomfortable and I tried to discover which muscle was

causing me so much bother. I twisted this way and that to find a position that would make my driving more comfortable. I got indoors, still in discomfort, went upstairs to spend a penny, came downstairs, sat down and then felt awfully strange. It was difficult to describe: more of a tightness in my chest than a pain, and although it wasn't severe, I was frightened by it. Something was happening to me that I couldn't control. Pam was busily knitting and hadn't noticed my distress until I said, 'I think you'll have to contact one of the partners. I don't feel well. I've got this funny pain. I think I've strained myself or something.'

'Oh, darling,' she said, looking up, 'you do look white. I'll give Steve a ring.'

Steve Maxwell was round in a few minutes. While he was talking to me and taking my blood pressure the pain eased away.

'I'm sorry to be such a bother, Steve,' I said. 'Messing about with that boat. I've called you out for nothing.'

'Bob, my lad,' he said, 'we can't ignore this. We really must send you to hospital and have this checked – and you are going in by ambulance.'

I couldn't believe my ears. This was what happened to *patients*.

'Are you sure?'

'I'm not sure of anything,' said Steve. 'But I want to be. You've had a chest pain, you're overweight, you smoke a pipe; this is a pain brought on by effort. I've got to make sure your heart is all right, and I can't test you properly here. It's Winchcombe for you, my lad, and the heart boys. If you're fine then you can come back and start work tomorrow but we've got to make sure.'

I felt all right now: the pain had gone but, looking back, I expect if a patient had come to me complaining of those symptoms, I would have thought he had had a heart attack.

I arrived at Winchcombe by ambulance, a new experience for me. The ambulance men, whom I knew, pulled my leg, saying, 'We knew we'd get you in the end, Doctor.' I was put in a four-bed ward where there was a monitoring unit wired up to a small television screen where I could watch my heart-beat merrily ticking along. The duty registrar came and examined me.

'Your electro-cardiogram is normal,' he said. 'We've just got to do some blood enzyme tests and keep an eye on you for a couple of days but, all being well, you'll be home on Monday.'

John Bowler, the physician, a great friend and whose overall care I was under, was away for the weekend. His registrar came in on the Sunday and repeated the ECGs. 'I'm afraid we're going to have to keep you a bit longer than I thought,' he said. 'There's evidence that you've had a heart attack. We'll know more when we get the blood tests back.'

'A heart attack!' I said. 'Surely not, Doctor!'

'Yes,' he said. 'I'm afraid they're no respector of persons.'

'But I feel perfectly well.'

'Good,' he said. 'That's the best thing you can do. But we'll get Dr Bowler to see you tomorrow.'

John came in on Monday and chastised me for trying to carry the boat on my back.

'Who do you think you are?' he said. 'Tarzan?'

Happily the blood tests were all right, but there were sure signs that my heart had protested at what I'd done to it, and there might be some underlying disease. I was to stay in hospital for a week and I was certainly to have some time off at home.

It was interesting being a patient, on the other side of the fence. I talked to the other members of the ward, one of whom was particularly ill and had had his heart restarted fourteen times, but was now doing well.

I had no further pain until the following Wednesday, when I suddenly had a recurrence. This was a blow. I rang for the nurse. I hadn't met her before, a rather grumpy staff nurse.

'Take one of these tablets then,' she said, giving me something to hold under my tongue.

'No,' I said. 'I don't want your tablet. I want the doctor who's looking after me, please.' I was a bad patient. She went out, snorting, in search of John. He came in and did further checks.

'Nothing to worry about, Bob, but we will have to have you on a regime. This won't hold up your going home but you've got to take it steadily next week. Start doing a bit more the next week, and from then on I want you really to start pushing yourself.'

It was nice to get home. I spent most mornings in bed where I could watch herons on the river, and salmon fishermen rowing out with their nets. With my telescope I could see that these men were enjoying good fishing, quite a different tale to the one they told when you met them: 'Very poor catches nowadays, doctor, we hardly get a thing.'

I felt well, I was doing an increasing amount of exercise and walking as much as two miles along the river bank in the afternoons, but I was taking a mass of tablets. Happily they seemed to work. What wasn't happy was that I would get chest pains at odd times. Whereas I might walk two miles along the bank without any trouble, I might get pain as I got up in the morning or when turning over during the night.

One evening when Ron Dickinson came for a meal I was boasting how fine I was. Then I walked upstairs and had to call him up because I had a severe spasm of pain.

I was due to see John Bowler for an exercise test a couple of days later. Pam drove me over to Winchcombe. This was going to be the crucial test. Did my heart protest when it was exercised? I had blood-pressure cuffs put round my arm and electrodes stuck all over my chest, and then had to mount a little pulpit. There were bannisters to hold on to and at my feet was a little treadmill, a conveyor belt. The last conveyor belt I had seen was in my mining days.

The machine was switched on and I started to walk along an endless 'path', holding the bannisters.

'Just imagine it's a stroll along the river bank,' said John.

As I walked John watched my ECG tracings. I had been going barely a minute when I began to get pain in my chest. 'Hop off,' cried John. 'That's enough. Come and sit down.'

I now had quite an unpleasant pain in my chest. A nurse squirted an aerosol under my tongue and in a minute the pain had gone.

'Have a cup of tea,' said John, 'and we'll have a talk in my office.'

John Bowler was the best physician I'd ever met. He was a first-class cardiologist and a general physician, as were most of the other physicians in the Winchcombe area, but he had an extra dimension. Somehow he was always able to see the whole picture of a situation. He liked seeing patients in their own homes. Patients loved having him call for a second opinion or special examinations. He was also a literary man and a great reader, in fact the best-read man I knew, with a huge collection of books.

He looked sombre in his office.

'Well, Bob,' he said, 'we have to face facts. I'm very conservative in my diagnoses, but you've obviously got extensive coronary artery disease. Nowadays there's a good treatment for it. It's surgical, and it's one of the commonest operations too. I won't minimise it – it's not a small operation – but it's very successful. If I leave you as you are, then you're not going to do much boating. Your activities are going to be very limited.

'First, we have to arrange for you to have a cardioangiogram [this meant inserting a tube into a main artery and threading it round into the blood vessels that supply the heart so they could be injected with a dye]. That will tell us if you need a coronary bypass operation. If you do, it involves taking a vein out of the leg and making three new arteries for the heart, bypassing any of the narrowed vessels that supply blood to the heart muscle itself. As Ron Dickinson says, it's the equivalent of having a new carburettor fitted.'

'You're the boss, John,' I said, with my heart sinking. I was worrying about being out of the practice . . . all my patients . . . how would the partners manage?

'Now stop worrying,' said John. 'If you'd been run over by a car they would have had to cope. Here's a chance of getting you back to full fighting fitness again. I'll make arrangements to get you up to the Middlesex Hospital in London as soon as possible. We don't do anything like this around here. In the meantime, if you can lose some weight, it will help you and them.'

I weighed in at fourteen stones two pounds at this time.

We had a pretty miserable couple of months waiting to go up to the Middlesex where an extremely nice physician did a cardioangiogram.

First I was well knocked out with an injection and from then on all I really felt was somebody pushing and prodding in my groin; it certainly wasn't a very trying experience. It meant my staying in hospital for two nights. Pam had come up with me. A friend from student days, now a consultant physician at University College Hospital round the corner, very kindly made his flat available for Pam so she could be near at hand.

My physician came the next day with diagrams and

drawings. It all looked awful. He pointed out the state my coronary arteries were in. He said that there was no real alternative but for a coronary bypass operation, but that I should do extremely well. There was quite a waiting list, but they hoped they might operate in about a month's time.

Those four weeks seemed endless, but many people have to wait for months. Things were made worse by the fact that I was having to try and lose weight. My diet was cut to the minimum and seemed to consist mainly of bran. Eventually the time for admission came and I went in on a Tuesday.

It was all bustle and activity in hospital; a physiotherapist came and explained what she was going to do to me immediately after my operation; my physician and surgeon visited me; I had chest X-rays, electrocardiograms, blood tests, urine tests, and was destined for the theatre on the Thursday. Somehow it didn't seem to bother me particularly – it's very much like boarding an aeroplane: you have to put yourself in the care of the pilot. An extremely pleasant grey-haired man and a very good-looking lady assistant came to see me to ask about height and weight. 'We look after the heart-lung machine,' they explained. One of the great advances in medicine is the fact that there is now equipment that can take over the duties of the heart during an operation. I made the mistake of calling the operators of this machine 'technicians' but they are the early members of a new society called the 'perfusionists'. However skilful surgeons have become, without these highly trained people most major heart surgery would be impossible. They also said that I wasn't to worry and that they would look after me. I could have kissed them.

I slept reasonably the night before my operation, was glad to have the pre-medication, then slipped off into a sort of limbo. I don't even recall the anaesthetist giving me an injection. The next thing I remember is waking up with bright lights in my eyes and a tube in my mouth that stopped me from talking. People were speaking to me and I was gesticulating for a pad to try and write messages. I was fully conscious or 'soggy' conscious. I seemed to have a fair number of tubes sticking out all over me. The front of my chest was uncomfortable but not painful. My left leg was bandaged and again uncomfortable, not painful.

Somebody whispered, 'His blood gases are all right. We can take this tube out.' The rubber tube in my throat was removed and I could talk.

The surgeon came and had a long chat with me, I gather only four hours after my operation. Our conversation I remembered quite clearly for days afterwards. The night was a mixture of dreams and night nurses. I was sick once which was unpleasant and I woke next morning in the intensive care unit. I was on continuous oxygen which meant that I had to wear an oxygen mask to keep my blood a bit richer, but I could take it off when I liked and have a cup of tea or other drinks.

Pam and Jane came to see me that afternoon and were absolutely delighted to see me over the operation and almost my old self again. But they looked fearfully at all the tubes sticking out of me.

The next day I was fully alert. The physiotherapist came and banged my chest every few hours. I then enjoyed a comfortable night and the following day all the tubes were taken out and I was sent back to the ward. Exactly forty-eight hours after my operation I was sitting up in my dressing gown having tea and toast. It was quite incredible.

I was encouraged that day to take a few paces. With the help of physiotherapy, over the next four or five days I increased my walking. The physiotherapist constantly enquired whether or not I was breathless or in any pain, of which I was neither, although my chest wound and leg did cause some discomfort. We reached a climax on the sixth day when I climbed two flights of stairs under her guidance.

'You don't need me any more,' she said. 'You're on your own from now on.'

I had cut down visitors to a minimum. I didn't really feel like seeing too many people, but all the children came to see me, as did Pam and one or two close friends. John Bowler did the round trip from Winchcombe in a day, just to see I was OK, and Steve Maxwell came up on behalf of the partners. The Scottish anaesthetist, who had a wonderful brogue, also visited me twice after the operation just to see all was well.

Throughout my stay the nursing was superb. The nurses were literally angels in white – in addition they all seemed terribly good-looking. I don't know who was responsible for their selection at the Middlesex Hospital, but whoever it was he had an eye for form. It was like waking up in the middle of a Miss World Competition. In spite of their good looks they were patience itself and nothing was too much trouble for them. When my heart gave an extra strong beat it wasn't always just because it had a new supercharger. I think it was related to whichever particular lovely happened to be dressing my wound, giving me a bed bath or whatever at the time.

I beamed a silent message to the spirit of Florence Nightingale for having got all this lot going.

What absolutely staggered me were the hours my surgeon and physician kept. I thought we were hard working in general practice but they seemed to work night and day. My surgeon would call in, often as early as seven in the morning before he started his list, just to see all was well, then again at night, perhaps after seeing somebody else.

'I haven't come to see you because you're ill or anything,' he said. 'I just popped in because you're a doctor.' He was a real treasure.

My physician, who was the gentlest and kindest of men with a great capacity for reassuring, for seven days called to see me every morning at eight o'clock. He was immaculately turned out, always with a fresh flower in his buttonhole. These two men, their team and John Bowler represented medicine at its highest and best; my only worry was that if they continued the pace of life, work and dedication that they did, they would all eventually be candidates for the operation they were performing themselves.

I had little pain. There were various preparations that I could have had for it, but they made me feel muzzy so I asked for something much milder which coped with the discomfort. The food was good; I had a small appetite but there was a menu and you could choose what you wanted. There was a TV in my room and when I at last felt well enough, I turned it on – straight into a film about cardiacs and bypass surgery in Australia, where apparently this operation is more common than having your appendix taken out. I switched off hurriedly. I had had enough of bypasses for a while.

The ten days after the operation did drag a bit. I had expected pain, but what pain I did feel was much less than I had anticipated, and I felt hot and a bit strange. The surgeon pointed out that this was my body reacting to the insult of being carved up. Nobody has control of his auto-immune system and it just takes time to settle down: the funny temperatures didn't matter. I was on various drugs to rid my body of excess water and keep the blood from clotting. Each day I was encouraged to walk a little further and be more active. My blood pressure and pulse and heart rates were monitored every four hours until the evening of the ninth day when the nurse came in.

'We're not bothering you tonight,' she said. 'You're off tomorrow.'

On the tenth day, they took all the stitches out, and there seemed to be yards of them. I had a very nice little line down the middle of my chest and a very smart scar the whole length of my leg. I was given the silkiest, most expensive-looking, full-length elastic stocking to wear for a time on the leg. Then home, glorious home.

The family were waiting for me with a bottle of champagne. John Bowler had apologised for not being able to welcome me home, as he was going that weekend to Yorkshire where his mother was very ill, but bless him, that first evening, at the end of motoring all the way from Yorkshire, up the drive came his familiar car. He checked me over completely.

'They've done a marvellous job, Bob,' he said. 'But just you make haste slowly. Ring me at any time if you have any problems or worries. Take it quietly for a couple of weeks, pottering about the house. From then on you are going into full training and there's no reason why you shouldn't be back at work in another ten weeks.'

I spent the first four days at home, just lying in my bed, thanking God that everything had gone so smoothly and so well, looking out over the river watching boats go by. I had landmarks in my progress, like my first bath and my first shower, and I started to come downstairs, gradually increasing my walking, going a bit further every day along the river bank until I was on a two-mile schedule again. It was cold and I had to wrap up warmly against the wind. I was two stone lighter than before the operation and I was determined to try and maintain my new weight.

All the partners came to see me. John Bowler popped in from time to time. Happily I had neither pain nor breathlessness and I now knew nearly every blade of grass along the river bank. I was due to go over to Winchcombe after eight weeks for a test to see how everything was working, and it was good to be alive. Pam and I, who are not really churchgoers, made a couple of trips to St Mary's Parish Church to thank whoever it might be that ordains the way of our lives for having kept a benevolent and kindly eye on me over these last few weeks.

CHAPTER 12

What the Stars did not Foretell

When I had been home eight weeks, faithfully doing my daily exercises along the river bank, I went for a check-up with John Bowler at the Winchcombe Hospital.

'We'll just see how the new plumbing is working, Bob,' he said. 'You've got to have an exercise ECG (electro-cardiogram).'

I remembered my last one, when I had lasted only a few minutes, and hoped to God as they wired me up that I would do better this time. I was slightly embarrassed because for some reason in this particular department of the hospital there wasn't a cubicle to undress in; so I just started taking my clothes off. I didn't mind this in front of John Bowler, but there were also a couple of technicians on hand. I was very conscious that, although I had lost nearly two stone in weight, I still had a few rolls of fat around the middle.

I mounted the conveyor belt, gripped the handles and started my walk. The pace increased, it became harder and harder work, but there were no bad results, no pain and I wasn't much out of breath.

'Cut!' said John Bowler, as if he were directing a film. The roller came to a halt and I hopped off.

'Fine, Bob', he said. 'Everything's working. You *are* unfit you know – your pulse rate was up in just a few minutes – but all's well. You will have to increase the amount of exercise you are doing. You can walk on the flat until you are blue in the face, but that's not enough, you must start doing some hills.'

I got dressed, thankful to have passed this hurdle.

As Pam drove me back to Tadchester, I told her about John's instructions. As we were experiencing one of our worst winters for some years, telling me to increase my walking exercise was like inviting Captain Oates to walk out into the storm.

Pam said, 'There's only one answer: we'll have to have a sunshine holiday somewhere.'

It wasn't as easy as we thought. To get a last-minute sunshine holiday at the beginning of February was nigh impossible. Finances limited us to a choice between Tenerife, Grand Canary, Madeira and Lanzarote. Southern Spain, the Algarve, Majorca or Minorca would have done for me but Pam maintained that she wanted a tan and had checked up on daytime temperatures.

We rang travel agency after travel agency. Nobody could find us anything before the end of March. We were joined in our search by Henry Long, a fellow 'walking-wounded' patient of mine who, a couple of months previously, had had a total knee replacement. We thought it might be a good idea to make a foursome with Henry and his wife.

When I had almost given up and resigned myself to thermal underwear and the beach at Sanford-on-Sea, a travel agent rang to say she had found us a holiday in the Canary Islands, which was not only first class but in addition was cut-price. It sounded too good to be true. We were guaranteed minimum four-star accommodation but would not know which hotel we were to stay at until we arrived at Las Palmas. We had to make up our minds straight away as the booking was for the following week.

I rang Henry Long to break the good news, but his wife, a former air hostess, would have none of it.

'I'm sorry, Doctor Bob,' she said, 'I've heard this story before. I never go anywhere unless I know exactly which hotel I'm going to. You might land up anywhere.'

Feeling mean, but knowing I had to follow John Bowler's instructions about getting some uphill exercise, I chided her for her lack of faith in human nature and travel agents, and booked the trip for Pam and myself.

We arrived at Las Palmas Airport in brilliant sunshine and high winds. A smart courier was efficiently herding people together in groups for different buses. We were to go to a hotel in the southern half of the Island. She gave us the name of our hotel, which meant nothing; it was not even in the brochure of the tour company.

In the half-hour bus trip from the airport our courier informed us that our hotel was one of the largest on the Island. This was encouraging. I've always thought of big as beautiful and I looked forward to breakfasting in bed in a sun-filled room, cutting a dashing, if scarred, figure by the side of the pool, and enjoying long leisurely meals in the dining room, where I would of course eat sparsely and go for the quality of the food rather than the quantity.

The hotel was huge. We were dropped at the door with the vague promise that there were porters inside; however at that particular moment they were all missing. We struggled to the desk with our cases. We were allotted room 795. The numbers went up to 895. We set off through concrete corridors, I dragging a heavy case which I'm sure was against doctor's orders, to find our room, which was as far away as possible from the centre of the hotel.

The room had been an apartment with a kitchen and refrigerator. The kitchen was now out of use and curtained off. We did have a sunlit balcony however – unfortunately, it overlooked a building site. With a hotel of this size, one end of it was bound to overlook a building site of some sort. The bathroom was shabby, with paint peeling off the bottom half of the door; the end of the bath was rusty and the bath and shower taps encrusted. Happily they all worked.

My ideas of relaxed dining were brought to a sudden halt. All the meals were self-service; room-service was non-existent. My anticipated leisurely breakfasts and dinners were replaced by meals eaten off trays after patient queuing. George Orwell obviously had a hand in planning this hotel: not only did you have to produce an identity card to get your room key, which was reasonable, but it also had to be shown when you entered the restaurant, where you were given further cards. If you were so indulgent as to order something additional to the set menu – for example, a glass of orange juice or a boiled egg for breakfast – it was marked on this card and you had to pay for it before you were allowed to leave the restaurant. Breakfast and dinner, which were served in the restaurant, were spread out affairs. Breakfast was from eight to eleven and dinner from six-thirty to nine-thirty, but during those times about sixteen hundred people had to filter those two points of entry. I wondered what Pam's father, Gerry, would have made of it all. I think he would have blown the place up.

Breakfast was a buffet of rolls, butter, jams, marmalade, cold meats and cheese, with purchaseable extras such as fried eggs, bacon and boiled eggs. Tea and coffee came from a press-button machine. For the evening meal there was a tremendous salad buffet, usually supplemented by cold meat and ham, and a vast array of various vegetables. A vegetarian's delight. There were two tables where hot food was available, meat and fish. On the first night I could clearly see that the meat dish was sausages and I was told that the fish was cuttlefish. There was no other night when I could identify either the meat or the fish.

When we ventured out of the hotel it was obvious that George Orwell *had* designed the whole area. It was purely a holiday centre, with hotels and apartments stretching for miles. There was no indigenous population, no local markets, no traditional or local work: it was all concrete buildings, supermarkets and shops that all sold the same things. The beach, twenty minutes away, was windswept with rows of umbrellas – not standing up, but lying on their sides as protection against the wind.

Our first purchase was a water heater and a small enamel teapot, which meant that we could make a life-saving cup of tea at any hour of the day or night. The only time we were unable to do this was the last two days of our week when – having then been three days without hot water and trying to heat a sinkful, as opposed to a teapotful – we blew the electricity in the room. Miraculously, the electricity was restored within an hour, but the water situation was not quite as bright.

From the third day the hot water stopped appearing; on the fourth day we had no water at all. As we had been advised not to drink the tap water and there were swimming pools to bathe in, this did not seem too much of a hardship. We were well stocked up with bottles of drinking water but what I had forgotten was that toilets need flushing. Being quick-witted I realised that it wouldn't be too long before our own bathroom became rather high, so I shot down to the toilets just outside the public dining room, to find that at least sixteen hundred other residents of the hotel had been even more quick-witted. The water was restored on the fifth day, and on the sixth day tepid water came through the hot tap, meaning that we could have a semblance of a bath before we returned to the UK.

I tackled our courier on 'minimum four-star accommodation'. She said 'This is the fault of the travel agents. They don't read the instructions properly. Four-star is no better than this anyway.'

Other indignant passengers had all been enticed with four-star promises, including one woman whose daughter was a travel agent and was quite sure that she was giving her mum a treat. Our hotel had firmly emblazoned on its front 'Three Stars', rather Spanish stars at that. Henry Long's wife was absolutely right.

The most irritating thing of all was that the hotel was absolutely ideal – ideal, that is, for somebody recuperating from a coronary bypass operation, who needed to exercise and not to put on weight. My room was exactly three hundred yards from the dining room and reception and there was no room service, so unless I wanted to starve or hoard food in my room, I had to walk a couple of miles a day just for food. The food was mainly salad and being self-service meant that there was nobody pushing you to eat anything.

We were twenty minutes from a splendid beach, splendid in spite of the wind, and there was an uphill climb back of a mile and a half. This was just what the doctor ordered, and, hurrah, it became a little easier each day. The sun shone, Pam got her tan and I came back confident, feeling fitter and for the first time after any holiday, not having put on any extra weight.

Apart from the basic accommodation offered by the hotel, other facilities were first class, but of course you paid extra for them. There was a very good independent restaurant, a steak bar, a beer bar, a disco, and a nightclub. For the young people there were plenty of activities: surfboarding, sailing, wind-surfing, water-skiing, snorkelling, swimming and tennis; and an abundance of nightclubs of the nicest possible sort.

In the brochure of another tour company, our hotel was described as active, lively and ideal for young people. I was lucky, but if Henry and his wife had come, it would have been a complete disaster for them and I would hate to think how anybody who was old and infirm would have managed.

I suspected that this hotel was a dumping ground for the other hotels, and that tour operators would fill up the four-star places and four-star-minus places and anybody left over would go to this monstrosity. Or possibly, as the hotel was so central, it was the other way round. I learnt a lesson, as Henry's wife had, that you are very vulnerable when making last-minute bookings.

For many of our fellow travellers, however, this was the holiday of a lifetime. If the main objective of the holiday was to get laid, this was the place to come. All the unaccompanied ladies on our trip – including two very elderly women – irrespective of size, looks or whatever, had all been very personally propositioned.

As we boarded the bus to return to the airport and home, an English girl who travelled out with us was having difficulty disentangling herself from a tall blond German in the hotel entrance. She eventually made it, and scrambled, breathless and flushed, onto the bus. Here am I, I thought, grumbling that we didn't get the four-star rating we were offered. I bet this girl would give this holiday a minimum of six . . .

CHAPTER 13

Back to Work

I came back after my Canary Islands holiday bronzed and raring to go to work. I felt stiff after my daily trips up the hill but felt I could cope with anything. I was quite happy to go back full-time but both John Bowler and Steve Maxwell said, 'There's no question of your starting full-time staight away. You've got to have at least six to eight weeks feeling your way back into work. You haven't practised medicine for six months; you haven't driven for six months: it's not going to be as easy as you think.'

They were very kind to me about my absence from the practice. It had put an extra workload on them all and had cost them money: they had insisted on paying me in full all the time I was away, as well as paying for the locums.

I started work again exactly twelve weeks after my operation. I was to do part-time until I felt I could cope with full-time duties again. It felt strange going back. Time did funny things: one minute it felt as though I hadn't been there for years, and the next minute I felt that it was only days ago that I had last seen a patient. Patients who were in ante-natal care when I went off, now came back with babies, but with most of the old regulars time had stood still. Conditions, conversations and prescriptions were exactly the same as before.

Most of my work had been covered by a delightful young lady doctor, Catherine, who had won the hearts of them all. I think secretly that most of my patients would have been quite happy to have continued with her, especially the local boys' boarding school. She was an excellent locum, though she only looked old enough to be a schoolgirl herself.

For six weeks I worked Mondays, Tuesdays, Thursdays and Fridays from about ten until six, doing no night calls or weekends. Then I went back to full duties, which presented all sorts of nightmares, and nightmares, by definition, come at night. At first I found it very difficult to cope with night calls: I had lost some confidence, and it was hard to gear up again to go back into action. I used to lie awake when I was on call, wondering whether the phone would ring, what the problem might be and whether I could cope. In my first few weeks back I was called practically every night I was on. One awful night I had four separate calls out. Gradually, however, things started to fall into place. I continued to get chest pains; they had warned me that I could for at least a year. I had to remember that my rib cage had been wired together, and that it would take some time to settle down. Fortunately, the ever-patient John Bowler would always be happy to check me over and say, 'You're doing fine. It's going to take at least a year before everything calms down. Your heart's fine and you've got a new lease of life. Make the best of it.'

In my early days back, I had an example of sheer unselfish courage. It was an urgent night call to a man with a heart attack who lived in an isolated country cottage. I left straight away, but apparently just after I had left the telephone rang again. It was the man's wife. She said, 'I feel certain my husband is dead. I do know Dr Clifford has had a heart operation . . . it's a long way to come . . . so, if he hasn't left yet please tell him not to hurry.' This was courage with a capital 'C'.

I had certain objectives. I wanted to have a break when I'd

been fully back at work three months and a week on the Thames in a cabin cruiser with Joe and Lee Church was just what the doctor ordered. It was a tremendous success, the ever-fit Joe leapt about doing all the heavy work while I steered the boat and Pam and Lee made sure we had a full table. I didn't even have to do the washing up. Joe and Lee were naturalists and gave another dimension to our holiday. They were always pointing things out – kestrels, lampreys and the like.

We travelled from Wallingford to Lechlade and back in glorious sunshine and spotted forty different species of birds in one day. If we hadn't had Joe and Lee with us I doubt if we would have noticed more than a dozen. We were chased into Eynsham Lock by the most huge magnificent cob swan whom we had fed the night before. It flew alongside beating the outboard engines with its wings; we were glad to see the lock gates shut behind us.

'He's a one, he is,' said the lock keeper. 'Think yourself lucky you're not in an open boat. He jumps on the back and plays hell. He just doesn't like engines.'

I felt much better after the holiday and gradually took over my full work load, though it did take at least a year for all my aches and pains to go. By the end of the summer I was trundling my boat up and down to the river – on the trolley, not on my back. Although my boat had triggered off my heart trouble, the problem had been there all the time. Carrying the boat on my back just drew attention to the fact that I had coronary artery disease. In a way the boat was almost a lifeboat: without its warning I could have gone on and had a major heart attack out of the blue. But I was caught before I had any heart damage and was given three new arteries. As Ron Dickinson said, 'You've got the best heart in the practice now – a supercharger.'

I was having a drink with C.P. in the Tadchester Arms about a year after my operation.

'You know, Bob, I reckon your profession's a damn sight

more useful than mine,' said C.P. 'Look what it's done to the two of us. We've both been given a new lease of life, by skilled dedicated men. I wish I'd been a doctor. My work means bugger all by comparison.'

'Rubbish, C.P.,' I said. 'We can't advance in medicine. All we can do is get better at keeping people alive, from then on it depends what they do with their lives. The only area that we can advance in is the arts and your work is invaluable; you're a communicator and the most skilled, humorous and articulate one I know. One of your fishing articles or philosophical tales will do more good than most of my medicines. Wordsworth said that a poet's job was to describe people's experience and enrich them by doing so. A writer's job is exactly the same. You give more help, comfort, humour and hope in your columns than you can ever imagine. What I do abhor about your whole conduct is the utter waste.'

'What do you mean, utter waste?' said C.P., looking bewildered.

I said, 'You waste so much time talking when you could have been drinking another pint.'

'Point taken,' said C.P. 'We'll have to find a pub where they serve quarts.'

CHAPTER 14

Family Engagements

After qualifying at Kingston – where one of his great joys was helping every week in the Citizens' Advice Bureau – Trevor went to Warwick University to do a master's degree in law. It was all very complicated and quite beyond my understanding. I wondered whether he might have preferred medicine after all, but when he helped me once to stitch up a patient in an emergency, it was obvious that he was not a natural surgeon.

He had an urge to write, and wrote very well. He was a beginning-to-end writer; he would sit down and shut himself away and write until he had finished. However, he had no success. He wrote at least two full-length novels, one of which was a rather strange book about a marathon for the physically handicapped, but he did show an ability. Home on holiday one evening he was sitting restlessly at a typewriter.

'I don't know what to write,' he said. 'I don't seem to be getting anywhere.'

'Why not try writing for one of the medical magazines?'

'About what?'

'How about,' I suggested, 'the problems of being a doctor's son?'

He hammered away for the next three hours and then presented me with the following manuscript:

The presumption that a doctor's son will eventually evolve into a doctor by some strange process which even Darwin could not have foreseen, is one that is accepted throughout the world. Even as a child, when the time came to re-enact the battle for Iwojima (or whatever other film John Wayne had appeared in on television the night before), I was always chosen as the first-aid man. This did not particularly distress me at the time because at least it meant that I never got killed, but I found little joy in treating my 'winged' cronies and missing out on the real action. As a protest one day I actually made a charge from the rear, hoping that one of the supposedly slant-eyed urchins from Up-the-Hill would shoot me in a way that would enable me to die like a hero. But the 'enemy' just stared at me with wondrous eyes and said 'You're not supposed to do that,' and I was forced to slink back to the rusty pram that served as our field ambulance.

My contemporaries were not the only ones who accepted this position. Whenever my father introduced me to one of his friends, I would invariably be greeted with the question, 'Going to follow in Dad's footsteps then?' In my very early youth, I would either mumble in the affirmative in the hope that I might receive a raise in pocket-money, or grin widely and make some precocious remark which my father had rehearsed with me the day before.

However, as I grew older, I began to notice things – the fact that my father frequently had to break off in the middle of meals, even on Christmas day sometimes, to visit a patient; the fact that at least twice a week he was called out in the middle of the night; the fact that he was frequently summoned to the door to stem the bleeding of a horrifically wounded patient who looked like an extra from a Sam Peckinpah film. All these things gradually put me off the idea of entering the medical profession.

I confessed my worries to my mother, and she seemed mightily relieved that she would not one day have to answer the phone for two doctors. My father, too, was by no means overcome with distress when he heard my decision. 'Good boy,' he said, tears of genuine emotion running down his cheeks. 'All has not been in vain.'

My rejection of medicine was helped by the fact that I had the least aptitude for science of anyone I have ever known. Having failed my general science O-level at Grade 8 after writing for three hours on the delights of the cuckoo pint, a career in either the arts or the social sciences was assured. As it turned out, law was the unlucky target of my aspirations. This was welcomed by all concerned as it meant that if my younger brother eventually decided to become an architect, there would be three professional men in the family. For my sister it was more difficult. As we all refused to let her join one of our own chosen professions (we were afraid she might do better than us), there were few professions left. My brother's suggestion that she might join the oldest one was instantly and very violently quashed.

One would have thought that my standing as 'the doctor's son' would be forgotten by my friends and relatives. True, my choosing of the law was a temporary haven, but unfortunately my father's patients still presumed that I was conversant with medical lore. Frequently I would be assailed over the telephone with symptoms of obscure diseases and my efforts to explain my lack of knowledge were usually ignored. A typical telephone conversation might run as follows:

Patient: Hello, is that the doctor?

Me: No, I'm afraid he's out at present, can I take a message?

Patient: Who's that?

Me: This is the doctor's son.

Patient: Oh! Well, you'll do. It's my daughter Rosie – she's got this rash on her bottom . . .

Me: Well, actually . . .

Patient: It's really painful and I was wondering if you could have a look at it . . .

Me: I'm not a doctor actually.

Patient: (after a long pause) But you said you were the doctor's son?

Me: Well, yes . . .

Patient: Well, that's all right then. Now this rash, it spreads right down her . . . etc. etc.

One can do nothing about fighting this sort of presumption and the only solution is to play along with it. Having been subjected to my father's telephone procedure from a very early age, it was quite easy to pick up such phrases as 'Where does it hurt?', 'Have you tried giving her an aspirin?', and even the word 'Yes' repeated in a thoughtful way at regular intervals. One can usually stall for time until they realise that you are an imbecile and ring off, or, as sometimes happens, my father arrives home, in which case I can say 'I think I'll hand you over to the doctor who specialises in these rashes.' I have even occasionally reprimanded a patient with the old chestnut, 'I wish you had rung earlier when these symptoms were first made apparent,' but my father has discouraged this as he holds the patent for that particular remark.

The crunch came when I actually had to help my father with a case. He was giving me a lift to the shops one day when a neighbour came running out of his gate, shouting that his wife had fallen over and split her head open. As was normal for a doctor's son, I remained in the car and laughed at the names in my father's appointment book, but after a while he came out of the neighbour's house and beckoned for me to follow him in. I obeyed, expecting to be presented with a cup of tea. Much to my horror, I found that I had to help my father do a temporary stitch-up of the lady's head. I won't go into details, but the operation took a lot longer than it usually took my father on his own. Afterwards the lady's husband said, 'I can see you're not going to follow your Dad.'

After that, word must have got round. When I answered the phone, patients would either ask for a proper doctor or even, on occasions, for my younger brother whose medical reputation was as yet untarnished. One lady who heard about the fiasco actually tried to report me to the British Medical Council until someone gently told her that, when it came to medicine, I was as much an innocent as she.

I am one of the lucky ones. To all other doctors' sons I have one message – Give in. Put down your towel, your spade or your briefcase and pick up a stethoscope because, whatever you actually want to do in life, everyone else will presume differently and there is no escape. Console yourself with the thought that perhaps, in the future, doctors' children will be presented at birth with licences to practice medicine – at least it will avoid a lot of confusion.

* * *

'I think that's excellent,' I said. 'I'm sure you'll sell it, but if it comes back, send it off to another magazine the next day.'

He posted his manuscript to a medical magazine. Four days later it was back. He posted it to *Pulse* the next day: within a week they had accepted it and paid him thirty pounds for his effort. He was an established writer now, being paid real money.

After leaving Warwick he lectured at the South Bank Polytechnic in London, but law and his conscience were not easily squared. He said that he could only consider academic law, as he felt that there were two laws: one for the people who had money and one for the people who hadn't.

Warwick University had encouraged his enthusiasm for acting, and now it began to show. In the evening he worked at theatres, behind the bar or as assistant catering manager, but the stage was obviously his first love. He lectured on law for two years and then announced: 'Dad, I want to be an actor. Would you see me through acting school? I've got to get this out of my system.'

'Yes,' I said, bravely (wishing he'd never asked). 'You've got to do what you feel you want to, or at any rate give it a try.'

I couldn't imagine Trevor as an actor. He had got rather heavy now and was certainly never very athletic. He had trials for various drama schools and, after a year, found a place in the Ealing Drama Studio. The bad news was that he couldn't get a grant. However, he was adamant that he would pay his fees.

So he arranged a loan with our friendly bank manager and I supported him for the year in London. I thought it was just a phase that would pass and he'd soon get back into law.

We saw several student productions of plays and I must say I thought he acted well. To our great pride he won, in the face of all the other drama students in the country, the first prize in the Carleton Hobbs Radio Award, which meant that as soon as he had finished his drama school he would have six months with the BBC Radio Rep.

He was busily writing at the same time but now his main themes were plays. He won the International Student Playscript Competition and was commissioned by Alan Ayckbourn to write a play for the Scarborough Theatre. New fields opened up for Trevor; he was always fully employed, sometimes in musicals, sometimes in plays. He would appear in bits of television and films. He played a prominent part in one of the Guinness TV commercials, and as well as performing in one of the Granada *Ladykiller* series, he wrote one of the episodes.

The family became Trevor groupies and would travel whenever we could to see him in his productions. I travelled out to the East End one night to see him play a major rôle in *The Ragged Trousered Philanthropists*, an old book long remembered, and did my parental duty by sweating through a three-hour performance of *Hamlet* on the top of the Barbican in a tent that wasn't properly ventilated.

In following Trevor around we discovered new towns that we had always meant to visit. We went to York to see him in *Having a Ball*, to the Aldwych Theatre in London for *Andy Capp*, to Chesterfield to see a rock opera. This was round about Christmas time and we took the opportunity of going as a family, Paul, Gill and Jane coming with us.

The day after the rock opera, we went to Dinnington, the old mining village where I had been a Bevin Boy. The Dinnington folk were still the marvellous, kindly people I remembered. They couldn't take us down the pit but they showed us round the pit top. All the children were fascinated by the mine and the miners.

We went to see my old landlady and her husband, Auntie and Ike Bradley, in their old people's bungalow. It was about thirty-five years since I had been their lodger. Pam had met Auntie and Ike Bradley before and we'd taken Trevor up when he was a baby. We went into the sitting room; there was Ike with Auntie Bradley in a wheelchair, she hadn't been well. There was a budgie, several generations removed from the one in my time.

Paul was the spitting image of me when I was his age. At the sight of him, Auntie Bradley broke down.

'There's our Bob,' she sobbed. The clock had turned back thirty-five years.

Paul and Gill had been going together for four years and Gill came with us on all our family holidays. Her father was now training horses, first in Hong King and later in India, and we used to see him and Gill's mother, Liz, a woman of great beauty, when they were home on leave. Liz was staying with us one Christmas, Eddie being stuck in India, when Paul suddenly said, 'I have an announcement to make.' We all stood silently with our drinks. 'Gill and I are going to get engaged.'

'Oh don't be silly,' said Pam.

'I'm serious,' said Paul, thinking his great moment was being stolen, but we had got so used to them being around together that we thought they were engaged anyway.

'That's marvellous,' we said. 'When are you thinking of getting married?'

'I thought 1995 would be a good year,' said Paul, jumping as Gill kicked him.

I don't know if it was something in the air or whether engagements are contagious, but for a time Steve Maxwell had been behaving rather strangely. For fifteen years he had lived away from the practice in a cottage on a smallholding, taking care of the retired senior partner and his wife and their younger daughter.

I don't know what he did in the evenings; he would never accept an invitation to a meal and never encouraged us to go and see him.

Fairly recently the old senior partner had died and Steve had taken a small flat in Tadchester.

Just after Christmas, one morning during coffee, Steve, who looked as embarrassed as I'd ever seen him look, and he must have been sixty-four or sixty-five at the time, said, 'I have an announcement to make – I'm engaged.'

'That's absolutely marvellous,' we said. 'For real this time, Steve? We remember your last engagement.'

Steve's last 'engagement' had been about ten years previously when a mental patient had tried to announce it in the *Tadchester Gazette*, but fortunately the proprietor had checked with Steve first.

There was some story, true or not, that Steve had promised the old senior partner that he would never marry while he was alive. He had been absolutely marvellous, taking care of the partner's ageing wife and sick daughter and now at last he was going to have some time for a life of his own.

He always took less holiday than we did; he used to spend a fortnight during the first half of the year putting the potatoes in his smallholding and a second fortnight later in the year, digging them up. He worked every Sunday. Perhaps things were going to change now.

He was marrying an ex-schoolmistress from an old Tadchester family who had a removal business and antique shops. Nancy Doone was a lovely lady, just right for Steve. What a waste that he hadn't been able to have a family and children of his own.

John Denton came into the surgery to have one of his many little septic cuts treated a few days later.

'I'm very pleased to see that Dr Maxwell is engaged.'

'Why does it please you, John?' I asked.

'Well,' he said, 'I've always thought what a nice young woman that Nancy Doone was and I said to a pal the other day, last week it was actually, "You know, I think that Nancy Doone isn't long for this world. She must be very ill. That Dr Maxwell's car is parked out there nearly all the time lately."'

Steve was a very private person – and to keep such a secret in a place like Tadchester, you had to be.

CHAPTER 15

It'll be All Right on the Night

For several years Pam had been a leading player in the Tadchester Drama Society, but this year she had opted out of acting to help found a junior branch, the Tadchester Youth Theatre, and direct its productions.

Though Tadchester was a lively enough town in the summer season, there wasn't much for the local youngsters to do after all the holiday attractions closed down in the autumn. The boredom this brought about had led to occasional outbreaks of vandalism and a few confrontations between juvenile or teenage groups. The Youth Theatre was a great idea for getting kids off the streets, and there was no lack of recruits. So many youngsters enrolled, in fact, that the problem was in finding parts or backstage jobs for them all.

The solution was a bumper Christmas pantomime with a cast of thousands – well, dozens – and C.P. helped with the script for *The Potty Panto Cavalcade*, a director's nightmare including characters from *Cinderella*, *Aladdin*, *Dick Whittington*, *Babes in the Wood*, *Sleeping Beauty*, *Mother Goose*, *Humpty Dumpty*, *Little Bo Peep*, *Little Red Riding Hood*, *Robinson Crusoe*, and with a Demon King thrown in for good measure.

Night after night, Pam came in from rehearsals worn out

and in a growing state of despair. The kids had not yet grasped the idea that there was more to putting on a show than just larking about on stage.

'They're not bothering to learn their lines properly,' said Pam. 'And the older ones keep nipping out to the pub for a quick one. Some of them are practically legless by the end of the evening. I shudder to think how the show's going to turn out.'

'Don't worry, darling,' I said, speaking from my encyclopaedic knowledge of showbiz. 'Shakespeare probably had the same trouble. It'll be all right on the night.'

I'm sure Shakespeare did have his problems. But if the first night of *Hamlet* was anything like that of *The Potty Panto Cavalcade*, it's a wonder there was a second.

The lights dimmed over the hushed audience, the front row of which consisted of Tadchester's leading civic dignitaries, with the Mayor and Mayoress in full regalia, chains of office and all. They were certainly doing Pam's company proud. In return, they were certainly given an entertaining evening, though Pam still breaks into a cold sweat every time she thinks of it.

One or two of the props had slight structural imperfections which had not been apparent at rehearsal, but which revealed themselves almost as soon as the curtain went up.

'*I'll cast a spell over all the land,*' said the Fairy Queen, confidently.

'*With just one wave of my magic – Whoops!*'

As she waved her hand, perhaps a mite too vigorously, the sheet-steel star shot off the tip, hit the stage and bounced into the orchestra pit, missing by only half an inch the jugular of the first trombone.

This brought roars of laughter and applause from everybody. Everybody, that is, except the first trombone, who sat there chalk-white with the 'Ffffttt!' of the spinning star still in his ears.

'Sheet-steel?' I said to Pam later. 'A bit robust for a magic wand, wasn't it?'

'I realise that now,' said Pam. 'But one of the boys is an apprentice at Turner's Metals. He volunteered to make the star and have it machine-polished until it glistened. I couldn't say no, could I?'

To the tune of *Jingle Bells*, the Magic Sleigh glided to the centre of the stage, pulled by two lusty lads in the wings, hauling on a nylon clothesline. The Snow Princess stood up in the sleigh, made a moving speech about the Message of Christmas, then declaimed:

'*Tis far away I now must go,*
'*To Santa's land of ice and snow . . .*'

This was the cue for the lads to haul on the line and pull the sleigh smoothly into the wings. They hauled a split-second too soon and with more power than was strictly necessary.

As the Snow Princess was curtseying gracefully into a sitting position, the sleigh shot from under her, dumping her ungracefully onto the stage, and careered into the wings. The lads on the rope overbalanced against the hardboard pine forest which masked them from the audience, knocking the thing over and landing in a tangled heap on top of it. Each loudly blamed the other in phrases which caused blushes among the gentler souls in the audience, and a horizontal fist-fight broke out.

The scenery was a problem all through the show. It had been made from whatever scraps the crew of amateur chippies and painters had been able to cadge, and was less than sturdy. It was a bit disconcerting when a castle turret crashed to the boards at an accidental touch from one of the Broker's men. And Peaseblossom's entrance was spoiled when her five-year-old foot felled the Enchanted Oak.

Dick Whittington rose to the occasion, though. As the Enchanted Oak hit the deck, he turned to the audience and observed:

'*My, oh my! Oh, what a fright!*
'*The wind is strong in the wood tonight!*'

The sound effects, too, made their contribution to theatrical history. The sound effects engineer, to give him his full title, was an eighteen-year-old who had only recently discovered the euphoria of alcohol. He had dived into the pub before the show for a few swift ones, made them a few large swift ones because of the pressure of time, and thereafter was not at the peak of his form. The result was that several times the cast seemed to be gifted either with extra-sensitive hearing or powers of premonition.

Buttons was explaining to Cindrella why he could not shower her with the luxuries she deserved:

'Alas, dear Cinders, I too am poor.

'Hark! Who's that knocking at the door?'

Whoever was knocking must have been using a sponge, for all the audience heard. Buttons tried again, ad-libbing desperately:

'Hear it, Cinders? Listen once more.

'I'm sure there's somebody at the door.'

Not a sound.

Buttons hissed to the wings for somebody to kick the effects man, and in a lather of sweat made one last attempt:

'Leave the jobs, Cinder. I'll sweep the floor

'As soon as I've found out who's AT THE DOOR!!!'

Knock-knock . . . came a noise.

Knock-knock . . .

Naturally, the door stuck as Buttons tried to open it. After a few frantic tugs, which left the door firmly jammed but threatened to bring down the whole wall of the castle kitchen, he called:

'The door is stuck. Alas! Alack!

'Whoever you are, go round the back!'

As Buttons peered expectantly to Stage Right, enter the Fairy Queen, Stage Left, waving her reconstituted wand ever so gently.

Abanazar had prop trouble, too, when the magic lamp failed to ignite. He rubbed and rubbed, but the disposable cigarette lighter in the spout just refused to function. Full marks for ad-libbers that night.

Abanazar saved the situation by saying:

'This magic lamp's not up to scratch.
'Has anyone out there got a match?'

Much more suitable for a family audience than the legendary old-time professional comic and amateur drunk who hit the same trouble in pantomime in Liverpool. His ad-lib was plausible, if not in the best of taste:

'Oh, dearie me! Oh, what a shame!
'Somebody's pissed on the magic flame!'

Just before the transformation scene which saw Cinders all dressed up for the ball, there was a clopping sound backstage which I first took to be another mistake of the effects man. But then there came the noise of an unmistakable and gargantuan fart, followed a couple of minutes later by an irritated 'Neigh!'

Thank God for the neigh: it illustrated to the coarser elements in the audience, who were still falling about, that the farting sound was not the product of the effects man, but of the Shetland pony borrowed to take Cinders to the ball.

The pony had been kept outside the hall in a horsebox until it was time for its appearance. Although it had been petted and pampered by the kids – perhaps *because* it had been petted and pampered by the kids – it was in a foul mood. The kids had been stuffing it with all sorts of goodies, too, from brussels sprouts to liqueur chocolates, which probably accounted for its digestive aberrations.

Led by its child owner dressed as a coachman, the pony stepped on to the stage, daintily picking up its feet to the sound of oohs and aahs from the audience. It drew a little trap, transformed with cardboard into a vague approximation of a golden coach.

All went well for a start. Cinderella climbed into the coach, arranged her voluminous ball gown about her, and sat down safely. Off moved the pony with a slow and dignified gait. Well, it was slow. It would have been dignified if the brute hadn't farted thunderously at every step, causing a few quavering notes among the orchestra and sending the audience into hysterics again. Finally it gave up all pretence to

good behaviour, lifted its tail and plodded off the stage, leaving piles of steaming dung at regular intervals behind it.

Thank God Pam was backstage, I thought. I don't know how I could have comforted her through the horrendous sequence of catastrophes. Not without bursting out laughing myself. But the Great Shetland Pony Disaster should be the end of it: nothing could be worse than that . . .

Towards the end of the panto was a scene in which the Demon King leapt out of a blinding flash and did a song-and-dance routine, waving his three-pronged fork and swishing his tail. Or rather *her* fork and tail: the role was played by one of the few accomplished solo dancers, a girl who had taken evening classes at the local dancing academy.

Whoof! went the powder in the flash pan. And out leapt the Demon King into the dance. It was at least a minute before she realised that her tail was on fire: whoever filled the pan had been over-generous with the flash powder.

Good little trouper that she was, the girl grabbed the tail

with her free hand and, without breaking step, tried to put out the smouldering end by banging it on the boards and bashing it against whatever piece of scenery she was passing. The waving about only made the tail smoulder more, though; and every time the waving stopped, the thing burst into flames.

Bless her, the girl carried on right to the end of the number. As she launched into the last, long note of the song, she laid the end of the tail on the stage and stood on it. The note didn't last as long as it should have done, but the girl had no trouble in reaching high C once the sole of her slipper caught alight. With a final screech, she leapt off the stage like a rocket and plunged foot and tail into a bucket of water proffered by an enterprising stagehand.

As I made my way backstage to comfort Pam after the show, I bumped into C.P.

'I'm sorry you've had so many disasters,' I said. 'Especially after all the work you put in on the script. I hope it's not spoiled the show for you.'

'Spoiled it?' yelled C.P. above the hubbub of departing patrons. 'Spoiled it? It's *made* it! Absolutely marvellous! We gave 'em Potty Panty right enough! Yes, those cock-ups have made the evening – I'm going to ask Pam how many we can keep in the show!'

'There you are,' I said to the white-faced and almost hysterical Pam, who was trying to sort out what seemed like hundreds of laughing, chattering and shouting kids. 'I told you it would be all right on the night . . .'

CHAPTER 16

Good Clean Fun

One of my favourite people in Tadchester was Philomena Fraser who, with her husband, Jim, ran a ladies' hairdressing business. The salon was always full, not just because Phil and Jim were expert stylists, but because there was always something going on to entertain the customers.

For anybody feeling peckish, there was a selection of Phil's home-made cakes. And on special occasions, a huge cake made by Phil's mother, Alice. When word got around that one of Alice's cakes was due, there was a sudden rush of bookings: no connoisseur of cakes would want to miss one of Alice's.

There was coffee, too, for the customers under the driers. And for those who fancied it, there was sometimes a dash of the hard stuff to give the coffee an extra lift. Few did not fancy it.

'Brazilian mild roast today, ladies,' Phil would announce. 'And if anybody wants it perking up, there's a drop of something all the way from Auchtermuchty. Hands up all those of Scottish ancestry.'

It was amazing how many females of Scottish decent patronised Phil's shop.

During term-time, Phil had to break off to collect her seven-year-old daughter, Laura, from school. Often Laura came back to the salon and entertained the customers with an impromptu fashion show or song-and-dance routine.

Laura had the best collection of stand-up jokes in the whole of Tadchester. 'I'll tell you a joke,' she'd announce, and launch into a non-stop stream of Christmas-cracker chestnuts that had the customers in fits of laughter.

Inevitably, now and again she would go too far and come out with a hair-curling blue joke she'd picked up at school. The fact that she didn't understand it herself was beside the point: it was that week's in joke, and she'd seen her classmates falling about when it was told.

'Right,' said Laura one day. 'There was this lad and he only had . . .'

When she finished there was a stunned silence from under the driers, broken only by a few suppressed giggles. Unfortunately for Laura, one of the customers was her paternal grandmother, Edna.

'Laura!' exclaimed Edna, shocked and embarrassed. 'I didn't hear that joke.'

'What do you mean, grandma?'

'You know very well what I mean. I *did not hear* that joke!'

'Don't worry, grandma,' said Laura. 'I'll tell it again. There was this lad and he only had a little willy and one day . . .'

* * *

On early closing day every week, Phil visited Tadchester Hospital to do the hair of the patients in the ladies' geriatric wards. Her time and skills were free; all she charged for was the wholesale cost of the materials, which came out of an amenities fund run by the Friends of the Hospital.

It was a great boost for the old dears to be fussed over and prettied-up once a week, and Phil's visits were always a great social occasion. She not only did their hair, she regaled them with a non-stop stream of patter and gossip which cheered them up no end and made them feel in touch with the goings-on outside the hospital walls.

Every so often Phil would get the patients involved in an Old Time Music Hall session: not just a sing-song around the piano, but a full-scale production in which every one of them could play a part. Even the oldest and most feeble was involved, helping to stitch costumes, making simple props or painting bits of scenery.

One old lady had been particularly troublesome from the moment she arrived. Given to imperious gestures and outbursts of disapproval at her surroundings and companions, forever hinting at a former lifestyle of wealth and luxury, she was a trial to the ward staff, visiting doctors and fellow patients alike.

'I hear you're trying to organise some entertainment for these people, Mrs Fraser,' she said during one of Phil's hairdressing sessions.

'That's right, love,' said Phil. 'Want to join in?'

'Ai should say not,' she sniffed, in a haughty and obviously counterfeit accent. 'Rank amateurs. Wouldn't demean myself.'

'How do you mean?' asked Phil.

'Surely you've heard of me? Florrie Farnham?'

'Florrie Farnham!' exclaimed Phil in a tone which implied instant recognition, but not having the slightest clue who Florrie Farnham might be.

'Florrie Farnham – the Tadchester Nightingale!'

'The Tadchester Nightingale!' exclaimed Phil again, still not having much of a clue but catching on fast. 'Of *course*! Just the kind of talent we need!'

'Well, I don't know that I've got the time . . .' began Florrie. Poor old love; like everybody else in the ward she had all the time in the world.

'Florrie – may I call you Florrie?' said Phil, who called all the other patients by their first names just as they – with the exception of Florrie – called her Phil. 'Florrie – you've got to *make* time. No matter how busy you are, you owe it to everybody in this ward, to all the nurses, to matron, to the doctors, to appear in this show. And if not for them, *please* say you'll do it for me.'

'I'll have to think about it,' said Florrie.

And that was that, until Phil's visit the following week when Florrie turned up for her hairdo clutching a list of songs, the appropriate piano arrangements, some demands for costume accessories and suggestions for lighting.

Phil, meanwhile, had done her homework and discovered that Florrie in her day had been a popular concert singer, never making the big time, but possessed of a good mezzo-soprano voice and well-enough known in the area to make a steady living as a soloist until her kind of repertoire went out of fashion.

I was invited to the Old Time evening and accepted with trepidation. The trepidation was justified by some of the quavering old voices which tried to rise above the out-of-tune piano, but I kept reminding myself that I was not there for my own entertainment. By the time the umpteenth chorus had bitten the dust in an off-key dying fall, I stopped wondering what I was there for and told myself it was all in a good cause.

Then Phil was up front announcing: 'Ladies and gentlemen – a very special treat for you this evening, a lady who I'm sure needs no introduction from me. The one and only Tadchester Nightingale . . . Your own – your very own . . . MISS FLORRIE FARNHAM!'

The little stage blacked out and was then lit by a single spotlight, which homed in shakily on a glittering diamanté tiara. The spot opened jerkily to reveal a magnificently gowned and amply bosomed figure which stood majestically with one white-gloved hand on top of the piano.

'*Velia* . . .' a passable mezzo voice began. And then gained strength and authority. '*Velia . . . oh Vee-lia . . . The witch of the wood* . . .' Suddenly the evening was transformed by the magic strains of that eerie song from *The Merry Widow*.

By the time Florrie had finished, I was blowing surreptitiously into my handkerchief. The rest of the audience, including the nurses, had no such inhibitions; tears were rolling down every cheek.

'Thanks again for a marvellous evening,' I said to Phil a few weeks later. 'I never expected to hear a voice like Florrie's. How's she behaving herself now? Less of a bother since she's been in the spotlight?'

'No chance,' said Phil. 'Last time I did her hair she was demanding top billing and a star dressing room . . .'

* * *

I doubt if many of the ladies of the geriatric ward would have survived the treat Phil laid on for her customers at the hairdressing salon: a visit to a male strip show.

'My own fault,' said Phil. 'I should never have had those copies of *Playgirl* in the shop. Before I knew it, they were all demanding to see the real thing. Women of the world, they said they were. Or hoped to be.'

So the trip from the salon was laid on. Thirty women, not counting Phil, and one man – the coach driver. Phil's husband, Jim, had wisely contracted out. He'd see nothing, he said, that he hadn't seen before, and it wouldn't do much for him anyway. He'd stay at home with his pipe, the telly and a bottle of Scotch.

Chattering and giggling, the women climbed out of the coach outside a club on the sea front which was plastered with garish posters advertising *All-Star Ladies Night! Positively No Gentlemen Admitted!* Phil checked the arrangements for the return trip with the driver.

'And what are you going to do while we're in there?' she asked him.

'Well, I've no other jobs on meantime,' he said. 'I'll just sit in the cab and have forty winks.'

'Oh no, you won't,' said Phil. 'Mrs Henderson dropped out at the last minute when her husband found out where she was going, so we've an extra ticket. You're coming in with us.'

Ignoring the driver's protests, Phil tied a headscarf over his bald patch, borrowed a spare cardigan from one of the stouter ladies, an ankle-length coat from one of the taller ones, hustled him into the throng, and before he knew it he was sitting at a table in the club.

When he took off the coat he was able to hide his trousered legs and boots under the table. Luckily the auditorium was dim enough for nobody to notice his five o'clock shadow, though the waiters must have wondered why the old girl in the cardigan kept her headscarf on all through the performance.

And what a performance! The respectable married ladies of Tadchester clapped, cheered, whistled in direct proportion to the amount of wine which flowed as the evening wore on.

'By heck,' said Phil. 'Those blokes! Especially Tarzan and the Viking. I'd seen nothing like it. Neither had any of the other women.

'Yes, there were a few red faces in the shop over the next week after they'd sobered up and realised how they'd carried on.

'But it did them a world of good. Women don't get nearly the chances that men do to let off steam and be a bit of a devil. They really enjoyed themselves. And, when all's said and done, it was good clean fun. Well, sort of . . .'

119

CHAPTER 17

First Aid Frolics

I remember clearly the characters in *The Wizard of Oz*: The Cowardly Lion who was given a medal which showed he was brave; the Scarecrow who was given a diploma to show he had brains; and the Tin Man who was given a heart. I shared their experience: I wrote a funny first-aid book and became an immediate authority on the subject. Once the label was stuck on me, I was an expert. There was no way, in spite of my protests to everybody, that I could not know all, and more, about first-aid.

In my first years at Tadchester, Gladys, who was then heavily involved with the Red Cross, had landed me with the job of medical officer to the Forward Medical Aid Unit. Each hospital group in the country had to provide a doctor, a trained nurse and ten auxiliaries, plus a van with lots of equipment, so that we could deal with the millions of casualties who would come down from London in the event of a nuclear holocaust. There was a national competition with the final four teams reaching the Albert Hall to be introduced to the Minister of Health. I was never, ever sure what we were supposed to do. Whatever it was, we obviously did it better than most others for our team was one of the finalists.

In time, all these units were dropped. Whether it was because the chances of a holocaust were receding, or whether it was on financial grounds, I don't know, but I would suspect that it was the latter.

My fame as a first-aider spread. I did first-aid phone-ins for *Women's Hour* on BBC Radio. They recorded a series of first-aid broadcasts I had done for them and sent it out on the World Service. For years afterwards I would meet people who would say, 'Oh, I heard you in Hong Kong,' or 'Guess whose voice I heard in the kitchen in New Zealand?' or 'What were you doing in Australia?' It's a credit to the frugality of the resources of the BBC that they kept this recording going round the world for many years.

My first-aid book was prompted by experiences of rugby injuries over the years. I remember the excitement of going to meet the great publisher. There he was, sitting behind a huge mahogany desk with Havana cigar, huge horn-rimmed spectacles and clutching an advance copy of my new shiny book. I asked tentatively when it was likely to be published.

'We have decided,' he said between puffs from his cigar, 'on Monday, the 17th of September. We have chosen Monday because on Monday more people read their papers than they do on any other day of the week. There's more book reviewing space on a Monday so you are more likely to get your book reviewed. All in all, books launched on Mondays tend to do better than books published on other days of the week.'

He paused, smiling wisely.

'Correct me if I'm wrong,' I said, looking hesitantly into my diary, 'but the 17th of September is a Thursday.'

'Great,' said my publisher without flinching. 'Thursday's a good day as well.'

It came home to me suddenly that the practice of medicine and the publishing of books had many similarities.

First-aid wouldn't let me alone. Apart from the radio, there was the yearly routine of giving first-aid lectures, attending first-aid examinations, offering first-aid facilities at agricultural shows, horse shows and point-to-point meetings.

Then came the big one: I was asked to produce six films on the treatment of home accidents and first-aid for Westward Television. This I did, thinking that soon I would be an international celebrity, but the films were quite terrible and I had the feeling that they burnt them after they had been made.

At the time, first-aid was beginning to take on a new dimension, not in the normal field like football matches, sports meetings and road accidents, but in the general deterioration of social behaviour. Violence in the streets had grown in every aspect of community life, much more so in the bigger cities, but these have their imitators even in the small communities. Over the years in Tadchester there has been a steady increase in the number of muggings, drunken brawls and aggravated burglaries. We aren't as bad as Winchcombe, Winchcombe isn't as bad as Taunton and Taunton is nowhere as bad as London. But anybody with a bit of knowledge of first-aid can have plenty of practical experience – patching up fellow members of the community who for one reason or another don't want to go either to the Casualty Department or the Police Station.

It is all terribly sad. Although we make great strides, or think we make great strides, for example in abolishing capital punishment and reducing corporal punishment, both of which being considered inhumane, it is now less safe to walk in the streets than it ever has been and man's inhumanity to man increases. It is as if every step society takes forward, it takes two back. I remember the advice given by three old men some years previously, when I asked them for a formula for improving society. Their joint answer was that no system could improve society, only better individuals could make a better society.

There isn't much new in first-aid. I strongly advocate it as a social skill to help cope, not only with the increasing violence in the community, but also with that other monster, the increase in heavy and high-speed traffic. Certainly a knowledge of basic first-aid helps to cut the toll of death and injury on the roads. Not only do people die because first-aid is not immediately available, but also they die because well-meaning amateurs actually harm them by doing the wrong thing.

Once I was just in time to stop a motor cyclist being killed by cod-liver oil. On a trip to see a patient I noticed a motor bike on its side in the road and a crowd on the kerb. From the house opposite was rushing a woman with a bottle in one hand and a spoon in the other. I stopped my car and pushed my way through the throng to find the woman pouring out a hefty dose of cod-liver oil and thrusting it in the face of the unconscious motor cyclist saying, 'Here, give him this, it will do him good.' What it would have done to him in his condition would probably have been to get him in the *Guinness Book of Records* as the first man to have drowned in cod-liver oil.

Drake's College, to which I was a medical officer, gave me a steady run of assorted first-aid injuries. There were broken noses on the rugger field and eyes poked out at fencing or gouged out at judo, and there was one boy who had a predilection for letting off fireworks in his bed, usually managing to lose a finger per firework. When he had managed to blow off three fingers, each in separate incidents, the school felt he should retire from his scholastic pursuits at this particular establishment in case he got over-ambitious and decided to blow the steeple off the chapel instead of a fourth finger.

We had been very lucky at Drake's College. As the system of management was changed, so the staff were increased. Whenever a boy had to go to hospital or to the dentist, one of the nursing staff would take him, saving his form or house master from being dragged out of school. There was a fine motherly matron, a doctor's widow, who was a great stabiliser for the whole school, boys and staff alike. Her assistant had been an outpatient sister at Winchcombe Hospital. In addition there were two first-class State Registered Nurses. They all had had children, and were familiar with the problems of boys and parents. They all knew a great deal more about first-aid then I did, and were able to take a lot of work off my shoulders – as well as always being able to produce a couple of dozen boys as really realistic casualties for my first-aid classes.

First-aiders really need to be of a particular temperament: they must be calm, reassuring, well-informed and terribly enthusiastic about their interests, but the main quality is calmness and not getting over-excited. My best first-aider, Barry Blunden, didn't have this particular quality. In my first-aid classes he did very well, both in theory and practice, as you would expect from a man whose secret ambition was to be a male nurse, but when the crunch came he proved to be a little short of self-control.

He was wakened one morning by a crash outside his house. From the bedroom window he saw a spinning motorbike in the middle of the road and a prostrate form in the gutter. Pulling on his dressing gown and grabbing his first-aid kit he ran out.

He weighed up the situation in a flash. Across the road was parked a neighbour's car and from the position of the bike, it was obvious that the rider had run into it.

'Silly bugger,' muttered Barry. 'What a bloody stupid place to leave it.'

A brief questioning of the barely conscious victim established the areas of pain. Barry diagnosed a broken left arm and possibly a fractured ankle. Swiftly and expertly he applied splints and bandages, only then did he turn and look at his own car parked outside the house. The back was completely stoved in and the rear screen shattered.

As realisation was dawning on Barry, the motor cyclist staggered to his feet.

'Thanks a million,' croaked the man. 'You saved my . . .' Just then his stricken ankle gave way and he keeled over. In an effort to save himself he grabbed the aerial on Barry's car and wrenched the thing off completely before collapsing back in the road.

'You bastard,' yelled Barry. 'Look what you've done to my car!'

It was a full minute before a neighbour ran out and dragged him away from the motor cyclist to whose ribs he was applying a tattoo of well-aimed kicks, certainly not a resuscitation technique he'd learnt from me.

The motor cyclist, Jim Ford, was one of my patients and after a few days he hobbled round to the surgery for a certificate.

'Sorry to hear about your extra injuries, Jimmy,' I said. 'On top of what you'd got, you could have done without having the boot put in.'

'It wasn't as bad as all that, Doctor,' said Jimmy. 'Thank God it was early in the morning. The mad sod had only had time to put his carpet slippers on.'

CHAPTER 18

Alarm Calls

I always rather dread the autumn term at Drake's College. It is the rugby term and we have many more injuries to cope with than we do in the other two terms. There is the intake of new boys which means about eighty routine medical examinations to perform and in every new batch there are usually a couple of boys with an undescended testicle that hasn't been noticed, and at least one who has not realised that he is blind in one eye. It is only rarely that something serious turns up. One particular case, a small healthy looking boy, worried the matron. I don't think she knew quite why she was worried, but worried she was, and I have a great respect for the intuition of those who have been in the medical profession for a long time; so often their suspicions are aroused not by logic or investigations but by an inner sixth sense that tells them something is wrong.

'It's his pulse, Doctor Clifford. It's a bit odd,' said Matron. This little lad had been under observation for flu, which was one of the other hazards that came this term. I examined him and I thought his heart had a murmur that ought to be further investigated. He was sent to John Bowler at Winchcombe who found that the boy had a serious condition: the main artery in the body, the aorta, was narrowed, the boy had very high blood pressure and needed urgent medical attention. Within a month he was up at the Middlesex Hospital in London in the same unit that had put me right. His main artery was operated on and his life literally was saved. If the first real symptom of this particular condition had gone undiagnosed, it could well have been this little lad's last. I was very grateful for my medical team.

No sooner do we get through all the medicals and follow-ups of medicals than the nursing staff have to cope with rounds of BCG jabs. Tuberculosis is only kept at bay by the routine screening of school children, testing them to see if they are immune to it or have come across it, and if not they are given an injection to build up immunity.

Autumn is also the term in which we give injections against flu. We have to have parents' permission for this and there are usually about half for and half against, and of the half for, the boys themselves say they are definitely sure that their parents have said no, so it often means rechecking, and for the half against, about a quarter swear that their parents have said that they should have it, so this has to be checked too.

Following the long break of the summer holidays, by the end of the term all the boys who travelled or lived abroad have to have all their immunisations brought up to date. This amounts to a good third of the school, so during the last month of the term there is a welter of jabs for cholera, typhoid, and a host of other diseases for which I have to write out certificates and prescriptions. And, of course, this is the term when flu epidemics, in spite of the injections, very often turn up.

Latterly the school has opened a junior school, not in the same premises but in the same grounds. This means that in addition to all the medical problems there are emotional traumas to deal with. As half of the eighty intake are little boys from eight to ten, there are great numbers of the wee chaps sobbing their hearts out for their mums before eventually settling in to this place of learning where they will probably spend the next seven years of their life.

The practice load is always heavy at this time of year, right up to Christmas, but the school medical workload is absolutely frantic. It is heavier in this term than in the spring and summer terms put together. I do three surgeries a week and during December it is like a countdown to sending up a rocket from Cape Canaveral. Whether it is matron or one of the sisters on duty at the surgery they say to me, 'Only seven more to go now, Doc,' then six, five, and so on until the last. If we make it to the headmaster's Christmas party and matron's Christmas lunch it means we have all survived another autumn term, but only just.

The year after I had my operation something was going on in the autumn term that was nothing to do with the medical examinations, BCG, flu or cholera injections, and it was something that was being kept from me. The headmaster and matron and sisters were grim faced; the chats over tea after surgery, although pleasant, weren't relaxed; there was something missing; there was something wrong. This went on for about four weeks. I probed as much as I could but they obviously did not want to include me in whatever trouble was worrying them. I was slightly miffed by this but just had to accept it. It obviously wasn't something medical.

It wasn't until the sixth week of term that I found a complete change of atmosphere. There was the headmaster looking himself, matron beaming and one of the sisters looking relaxed for the first time. On the table by the tea tray were three small cellophane packets containing white powder.

Good God, I thought, they're all on drugs.

Matron smiled, 'What do you think that is, Doctor?'

I picked up a packet and examined it – it could have been anything. From what I'd seen in films it looked like heroin or some other noxious substance of that order.

'Just smell it and taste it,' they said.

'I'm afraid I have no real opinion,' I muttered. 'I've no experience.'

I smelt it. I could smell very little. I tasted it and found it had a slightly soapy tang.

'What is it?' I asked.

'What do you think it is?' they said.

I said, 'I think it could be anything but I would suspect that it is a rather nasty drug that somebody is pushing around.'

'So did we,' they replied, 'and we've been in a terrible dilemma. We knew these were being pushed round the school; we didn't know what they were. We checked with various authorities for the likely signs and symptoms of drug abuse but we could find no boy who even looked as if he might be drugged. It's been a terrible worry. If we'd have reported it to the police they would have turned the place inside out. It was a problem we wanted to solve ourselves. We had the reputation of the school to consider.'

'Have you solved it?' I asked.

'Yes,' they replied. 'After failing completely to identify it in the laboratory, we had the bright idea of sending it to the public analyst.'

'And . . .?' I said.

'It's soap powder. We even managed to find the boys responsible . . . and the packet of soap powder. They were just showing off.'

'And,' said the headmaster, 'there are now four very sore bottoms which make this little escapade unlikely to occur again.'

Running a school isn't easy and I could see what a worry it must have been when those in charge thought that they had uncovered a ring of hard drug pushers in the middle of the school. I think I would have given the culprits a soap mouthwash as well as having tanned their hides.

*　　*　　*

There was one other major alarm in Tadchester at this time and it concerned my old friend Eric Martin, the proprietor of Tadchester Electrical Services. He complained of tummy trouble and said it was due to some frozen lobster he had for his birthday dinner cooked by the exotic Zara, his wife and Pam's best friend. The difficulty of having friends who are doctors is like being a doctor's child: you are either neglected or completely over-doctored. I am the over-doctoring sort so Eric was whisked to John Bowler at Winchcombe, in spite of the former's protests that he was quite better. As I had sent him and he was a friend of mine, John Bowler said he would have to have a complete check over. This meant not only chest X-rays, blood counts and a barium meal, but a barium enema which Eric said he wouldn't wish even on his worst enemy. Happily all his tests came back normal, only the barium enema remaining before he would be given a clean bill of health.

To prepare for his barium enema he had had to take some medicine the day before to ensure that nothing would obstruct the barium. The X-ray department posted the lethal ingredients – a packet of granules and two suppositories that looked like bullets in silver paper – and gave him an appointment a week ahead to attend Winchcombe for his X-ray. In the evening of the day he received this little parcel I had arranged to meet him with C.P. and another friend, Joe Church – a sort of sub-committee of the Tadchester Angling Society – to decide what we wanted to go on the agenda of the society's AGM. We were to meet at the Tadchester Arms at six.

On my way there I met the three of them in the street – they were part of a crowd of people who had been cordoned off by the police and fire brigade, standing some hundred yards from the Tadchester Arms. As I arrived an Army bomb disposal team turned up.

'Good God, what's happening?' I said. Up to that time the IRA had taken no notice of Tadchester.

'Some bomb scare,' said C.P. 'It seems bloody ridiculous to me.'

'Well, let's go somewhere else for our meeting,' I said.

'Come back home with me,' said C.P. 'I've got a few cans of lager. They'll only go stale if they're not drunk.'

We went to C.P.'s, had a bowl of his wife's home-made soup and settled down to our meeting. We had almost got it finished when there was a knock on the door from a very unfriendly-looking police inspector accompanied by a captain from the Army bomb disposal unit.

'Mr Christopher Parfitt?'

'Yes,' said C.P.

'Is there a Mr Eric Martin here?'

'Yes,' said C.P.

'May we come in for a minute?'

'Certainly,' said C.P. looking alarmed.

'Are these yours?' said the police inspector, holding out Eric's sachet of laxative granules and the cellophane bag containing his two silver bullets.

'Yes,' said Eric. 'Thanks very much. I must have left them somewhere.'

'Exactly,' said the inspector. 'You left them in the Tadchester Arms at lunchtime. At closing time the landlord found two bullet-like objects and a cellophane bag. With all these scares about explosive parcels being left here and there, he informed us and we had to bring out the fire brigade and the bomb disposal people. Unfortunately there is no way I can prosecute but by God if there was, I would.'

Eric looked a bit shaken and when they'd gone he turned to me.

'It's all your fault,' he said, 'I told you it was just that frozen lobster. None of this would have happened if you hadn't sent me to Winchcombe.'

Eric went off for his investigation the following week. I arranged to pop round that night to see how he had got on. All his tests to date had shown that in fact he was remarkably fit and this last one, although the least pleasant, was just a necessary precaution. I called at his house, was shown in by Zara, and found Eric lying white and shaken on the settee. I had never seen him look like this before.

'You all right, mate?' I said.

'What do you mean, all right?' said Eric.

'I mean, was your test clear?'

'Oh,' he said, 'yes, a hundred per cent clear; nothing

medically wrong. I told you from the beginning it was just that frozen lobster.'

'Well,' I said, 'you're looking worse now than you have looked at any time.'

'I know,' said Eric. 'They were right to get the police and the bomb disposal people out when they found that stuff in the pub. Those suppositories were just like high explosives. I'm sure I lost my tonsils as well as the rest of my insides. It has been at least four hours since I've been able to face a glass of ale.'

'Never mind,' I said. 'Think of the headlines for next week's *Tadchester Gazette*. It will read "Clear Out of Tadchester Electrical Services. Proprietor Flushed With Success Over Recent Inter-Departmental Investigations Has Wind of New Developments."'

I ducked as Eric threw a copy of *Angler's Mail* at me.

CHAPTER 19

Wedding Bells

Jane's A-level years passed only too quickly, though perhaps not for her. She went through all the bitter-sweet agonies of adolescence; her hair changing colour right through the spectrum in the search to find the magic colour. From a lovely, fair, auburn shade it progressed finally to jet black which, when she viewed it in the mirror for the first time, made her burst into tears. She was not helped at all when Mick Brown, one of Paul's entourage, wisecracked on his first sight of her, 'I didn't know Betty Boop lived here! She looked quite different, black. Growing it out was a long painful process, and she settled in the end for having her hair sort of half-dyed.

She also seemed to wear clothes that didn't suit her at all, enraging the headmaster of her comprehensive school who always included a note on her report about her bizarre dress and colouring.

At last she sat through the dreaded torture of A-levels, passed, and secured a place on a foundation course in art at Brighton Polytechnic. Almost before we'd realised it, she was off to Brighton and we were down to a household of three; Pam, myself and Paul. Not that Paul really counted as a full-time resident: home was just a place where he stored all his amplifying gear and rested in between work and gigs.

Jane loved Brighton, worked hard in her first year, then moved on to a three-year degree course on the history of design. She came home whenever she could, to watch Trevor in whatever new play he was in, and go and shout for Paul's group whenever it played within spitting distance.

Paul and Gill's engagement didn't seem to make much difference to their relationship; they just seemed to go on as before. Whenever Paul was asked when they were likely to get married, he'd say, 'I've only two stipulations: it mustn't be on the day of the Cup Final, and Trevor must be best man.'

Suddenly, Paul and Gill had to get married in a hurry. Not for the usual Tadchester reason but because both Gill's mother, Liz, and father, Eddie, lived in India and they only came home for a few weeks in the spring of each year. Gill wanted her parents at her wedding, and if it wasn't this particular spring, it would have to be the next one.

By now, Paul was working little on his music, but was trying to write. His job in the electronics factory had no real prospects and he had ambitions to be a sports writer. Gill was a marvellous cook, an accomplished painter, had qualified in an arts course and designed and made jewellery. Her parents in India, she had to arrange her own wedding. She rushed round organising invitations, receptions, wedding dress.

'Good God,' said Paul, 'I never realised getting married was so complicated.'

He was happy with the arrangements, however. The wedding date didn't clash with the Cup Final, Trevor turned down a part in a play to be his brother's best man and Jane was to be a bridesmaid. But to add to the activity, Gill's sister and her fiancé, taking a leaf from Gill's book decided to marry a week after Gill and Paul.

Poor Liz and Eddie were going to lose two daughters in a week, and Liz flew home from India early to help sort things out.

I took Paul on one side to give him some fatherly advice:

'The first thing, Paul, is don't refuse anything anyone offers you, however grotesque, be it a three-legged chair or a one-legged stool. If you turn it down, they'll never, never, give you anything else.'

They were fortunate that they were able to find an end-of-terrace cottage with garage and out-buildings and in a lovely setting. It was two hundred years old and just the place for Gill to do her jewellery and metalwork.

The weather prospects for the wedding day looked poor. It had been a cold, wet and miserable spring. They were to be married at St Mary's Parish Church in Tadchester, with a reception at the Port Vere Hotel, five miles away. This was an old country house set in acres of landscaped gardens with its own private beach. In the evening everybody was coming back to us for a party. Paul and Gill were to spend the first night of their honeymoon in Taunton, then fly off to Paris the following day.

At last the great day arrived. The indefatigable Mick Brown, who was taking a video of the wedding, was up filming from the crack of dawn. He videoed Gill washing and having her hair done, managed to catch Jane in bed, and went on to film the whole ceremony, reception and going-away in the evening. The gods looked kindly on us; this was the one fine day in the midst of an awful spell.

Gill looked like a princess in a dress which she designed herself. Paul and Trevor looked splendid, tall and for once well-groomed in their hired attire. The church was packed. As well as a hundred guests, there were patients who had known Paul since he was a baby. Catherine, my stand-in, very kindly covered the surgery for the day and all the partners turned up. Ron Dickinson distinguished himself by starting the celebrations long before the wedding began. While the photographs were being taken in the churchyard, he decided to make an unescorted, unroped attack on the south face of the church spire. No sherpas or oxygen either, though he looked as if he could have done with both by the time he came down.

The boys made impressive speeches at the reception. Paul

wasn't going to be outdone by his actor brother and Trevor not only welcomed Gill into the family but also her incontinent cat, which was going to be boarded with us while they were on their honeymoon.

Pam's brother, Theo, who has the energy of at least three men and spends his life shooting round the world opening more and more companies, organised the rest of the afternoon's entertainment when we arrived home after the reception.

'Come on, lads,' he said, 'it's the cricket season.'

It must have been one of the few games of cricket played in morning dress. The bride, her beautiful white creation tucked into her waist, took her turn at batting like everybody else.

There was eating and drinking and talking and kissing. Relatives that we only saw at funerals and weddings were all saying to each other and to us that we must get together more often. Then, finally, there was Mr Sparks, the taxi man, at the door, ready to take Paul and Gill off on their honeymoon. Mick Brown had organised floodlighting of the whole of the area outside the house so he could video their departure. Then, with shouts, cheers, kisses and goodbyes, they were away at last.

One hour later Mick Brown was back with the video of the wedding and we had a three-hour replay of all the day's proceedings.

The eating and drinking went on for a couple more hours. The guests and relatives that were staying with us went to bed and Pam and I were left sitting in the lounge. Suddenly the house was deathly quiet. Pam looked up at me.

'Darling,' she said, 'I've something to say to you.'

'Are you thinking what I'm thinking?'

'Yes,' she said. 'Life is going to be different from now on.'

Postscript

There is the fable of the old man sitting outside a town, being approached by a stranger.

'What are they like in this town?' asked the stranger.

'What were they like in your last town?' replied the old man.

'They were delightful people. I was very happy there. They were kind, generous and would always help you in trouble.'

'You will find them very much like that in this town.'

The old man was approached by another stranger.

'What are the people like in this town?' asked the second stranger.

'What were they like in your last town?' replied the old man.

'It was an awful place. They were mean, unkind and nobody would ever help anybody.'

'I am afraid you will find it very much the same here,' said the old man.

If it should be your lot to ever visit Tadchester, this is how you will find us.